THE SHOPS

The Shops

India Knight

VIKING
an imprint of
PENGUIN BOOKS

VIKING

Published by the Penguin Group

Penguin Books Ltd, 80 Strand, London, WC2R ORL, England

Penguin Putnam Inc., 375 Hudson Street, New York, New York 10014, USA

Penguin Books Australia Ltd, 250 Camberwell Road,
Camberwell, Victoria 3124, Australia

Penguin Books Canada Ltd, 10 Alcorn Avenue, Toronto, Ontario, Canada M4V 3B2

Penguin Books India (P) Ltd, 11 Community Centre,
Panchsheel Park, New Delhi – 110 017, India

Penguin Books (NZ) Ltd, Cnr Rosedale and Airborne Roads,
Albany, Auckland, New Zealand

Penguin Books (South Africa) (Pty) Ltd, 24 Sturdee Avenue,
Rosebank 2196, South Africa

Penguin Books Ltd, Registered Offices: 80 Strand, London, WC2R ORL, England

www.penguin.com

First published 2003

I

Text copyright © India Knight, 2003
Illustrations copyright © Sam Wilson, 2003

The moral rights of the author and illustrator have been asserted

Set in Mrs Eaves
Design and typeset by Smith & Gilmour, London
Printed in Great Britain by Clays Ltd, St Ives plc

A CIP catalogue record for this book is available from the British Library

ISBN 0-670-91373-1

To Amaryllis and Afsaneh

No man is rich enough to buy back his past.
OSCAR WILDE

I take Him shopping with me.
I say, OK, Jesus, help me find a bargain.
TAMMY FAYE BAKKER

Contents

Introduction   1

Beginning   7

Big Fat Dinners   31

Looking Better   66

Nests   102

Home   118

Wedding Dress   145

Mothers and Children   158

Presents   173

How to Shop   196

'Our Lady of Pleasure'   201

Acknowledgements   208

Index   209

Where shops have several branches, the address, telephone number and opening times given usually refer to the largest and/or flagship store. And while every effort has been made to provide up-to-date addresses and telephone numbers, and e-mail and website details, obviously these can change, so beware!

Introduction

This is not a shopping guide; it's a book about shopping — a sort of *Joy of Sex* for shops, with fewer beardy, tumescent men. It's not going to tell you to go to blissful Peter Jones — although obviously you should, often — to buy wool (and bamboo knitting needles, a revelation after using metal) or hosiery. It's not going to direct you to Harvey Nichols, because it assumes that you know where it is, and what it's for (footballers' wives. Only joking! It bee a big fancy shop in that there Lunnun). There are no great long lists of stores I think you ought to frequent, but, scattered here and there, there *are* incidental boxes. I am extremely pleased with these boxes. They contain gems: the very best shopping addresses I have gathered in the course of my research. Yes, I've done shopping research — imagine the hardship: the oil-rig worker, the junior doctor and me, slaving away at the coal face, bloody but unbowed.

Actually, I've been researching this book throughout the course of my adult life, because shopping has been my hobby — my vocation, almost — since I was a very small child. Hence the boxes: I am sharing my shopping Good News, evangelically. You want pants that'll take two inches off your waist without (crucially) redistributing the podge on to your lower back or — eeooo — upper thighs? You want cream that gets rid of snog-rash? Cherry cake to swoon over? A country cottage to rent for half-term? Look in the boxes. They ought, for the most part, to be helpful wherever you live, thanks to the goodness of online shopping and mail order. It goes without saying that they are also completely and necessarily subjective: don't blame me if you order gingerbread and then don't like the taste, or if you don't share my definition of a good facial. And please don't misinterpret this book as some sort of creepy guide to gracious living — buy what I buy, live like me

— because I am the kind of person who eats bacon sandwiches in the bath, can spend days shunning human contact in favour of Georgette Heyer, and would rather count the hairs on my head one by one than even *think* about amusing new ways with place setting/floral arrangements.

But I do love the shops. Oh, God, The Shops. I can't quite remember if that almost-not-daring-to-believe, kick-in-the-stomach feeling of pure joy — 'You mean we give you a few coins and the lovely thing becomes mine?' — first happened when my paternal grandmother took me to a *pâtisserie* (Vatel in Brussels, 8 rue General Leman — they still do absolutely the best baguette in town), where I stood transfixed in front of a tiny *tartelette au citron*: pale yellow, with frilled edges and *Citron* written (just like that) in tall, thin, curly letters of darkest chocolate. I don't think I'd quite grasped that food came from shops before (sheltered childhood, and I was only six), and this *tartelette* was a revelation. The idea that you could eat delicious things all the time, if you liked, simply by taking a few steps down the street and SHOPPING, was just amazing to me.

So that's where the passion started, I *think* — either then or perhaps sometime the same year, in the giant *papeterie* on the rue Belliard, around the corner from my grandparents' flat. A *papeterie* is a stationer's, stupidly prosaic in English — the word really deserves a better, more lyrical, more ecstatic translation. I love paper, and this is where the love began. This hushed, sober shop had, obviously, paper by the quire: thin paper, thick paper, hand-made paper, marbled paper in six shades of pink, like melting strawberry ice-cream — and coloured inks, and heavy, solemn, important-feeling fountain pens, and felt tips, nibs, quills, woody pencils with rich, oily leads (mmm, graphite), rows of beautifully bound books with hopeful blank pages . . . We'd gone to buy me some Caran d'Ache pencils. I remember the shop's smell to this day, and the sort of swoon I fell into by the counter; I remember my grandfather's complicit smile — the

smile of recognition of like meeting like: he, too, was a stationery fetishist (he also taught me how to stand in bookshops, appreciatively sniffing the air before diving in – this was in the days when bookshops were small and didn't smell of Starbucks).

I still spend a disproportionate amount of time in my local stationer's, groping the very ordinary notebooks, sometimes quite wanting to lay my cheek on their pristine pages. I also go to artists' supply shops and stand in a corner, beaming with love at the brash, jaunty tubes of acrylics, the tiny, elegant blocks of watercolour, the sable brushes – and, of course, the paper. I got my eldest son his own big box of Caran d'Ache pencils recently, and became somewhat teary-eyed as I was buying them. One of the funny things about shopping – and I'll get to this in a later chapter – is that it can dredge up the most unexpected emotions, especially if you're comfort-shopping, which is to say usually shopping for some aspect of your mislaid childhood.

Possibly this little explanation concerning the origins of my passion says more about my greed or northern European ploddiness – cakes, paper, *ist gut, ja?* – than about my love of shopping, but then if you love shopping as I do, a lemon tartlet or a notebook can send you into the same throbbing ecstasies as a cashmere coat, even in adulthood. A washing-up brush can become the acme of desirability if it is the *right* washing-up brush (round, wooden, real bristles = good, quite want to do the washing up; speckledy grey plastic = horrible, what am I, your domestic slave?).

Hence the boxes: I've shopped a lot. In recent years, I have also become obsessed with the magic of online shopping. You have to kiss a lot of frogs, but eventually you find a real prince of a shop (the princes – and quite a few kings – are in the boxes). You sit there in your pyjamas, click a few buttons with your wee mouse, and a few days later a wonderful, thrilling parcel arrives. There is a such a special delight in opening a parcel, tearing through the cardboard, feeling like you've got a fabulous, perfect present from someone who knows you really well. Which, in fact, you have. Only yesterday a lovely pistachio-and-violet-coloured suede backgammon board arrived from an online shop* (*and it was cheap*), which probably explains my good mood today. Hell being other people, you don't get a mood like that from schlepping up and down Oxford Street on a Saturday afternoon.

So, I'm not here to tell you how to dress (though I've included some foolproof tips for how to dress if you're size 14 or above, because I'm fed up with perfectly normal women wandering about all hunched and slopy, wearing giant smocks, looking like ashamed puddings), or where to buy your food from (though I've passed on a few ideas), or how to get a digital camera at bargain-basement prices – try one of those guides to Internet shopping instead. What this book is for is to try and explain why it is that shopping is such a joy (and to try and convert those who disagree, poor fools), and to find out what it is we are actually doing, actually hoping for, actually *saying* when we pop down The Shops. Oh, and did I mention the boxes?

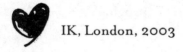 IK, London, 2003

---

* From Plumo, to be precise – see www.plumo.co.uk.
They also do very charming tins and excellent cushions.

Beginning

It saddens and amazes me that there are people out there who actually hate shopping. Men, for instance, are traditionally supposed to be hopeless at it: grumpy and monosyllabic when lured down the high street, wishing they were at home browsing the web for gadgets instead. Now, I don't want to come over all American self-help manual here (pity — I'd probably have a best-seller on my hands if I did: *Because You're Worth It — How to Shop for the Self within You*), but hating shopping is a terrible accident. It happens to people who've never shopped properly, and allow one bad experience to contaminate and sully the rest of their shopping life. It is extremely sad, a) because it just is and b) because we all *have* to shop, whether we like it or not. So we may as well like it. Even heterosexual blokes.

I can see how it happens, though, shop-hatred. Devoted as I am to my number one hobby, it would be plain foolish not to admit that some shopping experiences are absolutely hellish. I mentioned Oxford Street on a Saturday afternoon in the introduction: swarms of people not knowing what they want but knowing they want it badly, milling around like grubs (I'm mixing my metaphors, but they're all to do with insects, you'll notice); the smell of cheap burgers; the rustle of nyloned thigh meeting nyloned thigh; the sense of despair; the grotesque, palpable greed . . . Yes, it's hell. But this scenario has as little to do with true shopping as a drunken fumble in an alleyway with a man who looks like a pig has to do with a weekend at the Ritz with the one you love. We'll get to that later. We'll make every shopping experience as far removed from the icky fumble as is humanly possible. It's not difficult when you know how — but it's not necessarily easy to know how, either. For many of us — well, many of *you* — shopping is simply bewildering. It promises, but it doesn't deliver. There is a literal embarrassment of choice. And so shopping becomes joyless.

But first we need to go back to the beginning. Where does it come from, this delight in The Shops? Is it inherited? Is there a shopping gene? Certainly, my mother was – and remains – a champion shopper. But, possibly because of her ultra-luxe tastes, when I was a child she shopped in a very different way from me. Put simply, I like tat and the romance of tat – of stupid, pointless, lovely, glittery cheap things – and she doesn't. She didn't shop very frequently, but when she did, you knew about it. I shop little and often, a method I strongly recommend.

When I was a small girl, growing up in Brussels with frequent exeats to Paris, we seemed to be either improbably rich or improbably hard up, with no in-betweens. My parents separated when I was two, and my mother and I lived by ourselves in a (for the time) freakily minimalist apartment on the Avenue de Tervuren. My mother, a designer who is blessed with a most extraordinary 'eye', has always had minimal tastes, and so there we were, with acres of bareness (lack of funds may have contributed to the overall look), the odd exquisite *objet* and a fascinating textured blue rubber floor that looked like giant bubble wrap in our kitchen. We ate porridge when we were broke, which was about half the time, and tins and tins of sardines ('full of protein', though I think the aesthetic aspect – the beautiful retro Spanish and Portuguese labels on the tins – had as much to do with it as the nutritional one). When we weren't broke . . . well, my mother tells a story which I think I am supposed to be obscurely flattered by, which in reality I find crippling, but which I pass on anyway in the spirit of explanation. I was aged about five, and she about twenty-three, and we were in an upmarket Brussels supermarket called Rob – a kind of Belgian Fortnum's, now defunct – and as we were queuing up to pay, she remembers me panickedly telling her, at the top of my voice, that we'd forgotten the caviare: *Maman, maman, on a oublié le caviare*. One can only imagine the delight of the other shoppers.

A SHOP IN BRUSSELS

There are lots of shops in Brussels, obviously, and lots of
chocolates, but the former are Euro-standards* and the latter
feature in the chapter on food. The one place I absolutely always
make a beeline for, if only to drool, is Delvaux, makers of supremely
elegant, well-constructed, ultra-chic, ultra-pricey handbags (and
leather goods) since 1829. My grandmother and all her sisters
cherished theirs, gazing sniffily at lesser bags, and it is true that a
Delvaux bag is like a family heirloom. These are instant classics,
made with unusual amounts of care and precision, perfectly
designed, so impeccable that other bags somehow start looking
pitifully shoddy by comparison. You can tell from little things: only
Delvaux and Hermès still use continuous stitching for their bags,
for example (examine your handbag. There are little knots where the
manufacturer has used up a bit of thread. If the thread is cheap, it
eventually starts fraying. Continuous stitching means the same,
high-quality thread all the way round the bag, and no little knots or
uprisings of thread. This also applies to cashmere: you only get
pilling if cheaper, short threads have been used). The leather is
unbelievably soft and the muted colours are beautiful. This is real
understated luxury – unless they're Belgian, no one knows about
Delvaux much, though there are a handful of Delvaux shops in the
States – ideal if you're a bit of a bag fetishist but hate the idea of
anything glitzy and covered in ghastly logos, and care deeply about
quality. The bags really do last a lifetime, or two or three, and are
outside fashion. A diffusion line, Le Deux, is marginally cheaper
(which isn't saying much) and trendier. But trendiness isn't
really the point. The shops are at 27 Boulevard de Waterloo
(+ 32 2 513 0502) and 31 Galerie de la Reine (+32 2 512 7198).

 * If you want cutting-edge clothes (or, tra la la, diamonds), go to
Antwerp and stay at a hotel called De Witte Lelie – ten heavenly bedrooms
on a seventeenth-century canal, exceptionally delish breakfasts.
See www.dewittelelie.be, or call: +32 3 226 1966.

So that was my mother: feast or famine. Sardines with crunchy,
spindly bones or Beluga for two. I have no recollection whatsoever
of buying Jif or loo paper or potatoes with her, though surely we
must have done. All my shopping memories of my mother involve
things like haring around looking for Alfonso mangoes (they're
only in season for one month); buying hundreds of postcards of
the head of Nefertiti when the Tutankhamun exhibition hit
Brussels in the 1970s; and buying clothes.

Ah, the clothes. We were very well dressed, my mother and
I (she still is. I am writing this in fleecy pyjama bottoms and an
ancient, dog-smelling jumper). When she married my stepfather
and we came to live in England, in crazy, beyond-parody 1970s
Islington (in Sisterwrite, the local bookshop, an alarm bell
sounded if a man walked in), I remember one of the mothers of
the children on the square talking disapprovingly about my 'funny
French clothes'. Even then, aged ten, I felt some pity for the
woman in question, rather than any deep sense of hurt for myself:
dungareed, braless and make-upless, with hair like rats' tails — to
say nothing of a crashing lack of manners — I knew she could really
have benefited from my clothes-related (and, by this time,

CHILDREN'S CLOTHES

You know how it is: you want them to wear sweet old-fashioned triangular dresses and children's Birkenstocks;* they want clicky-clacky Barbie mules and T-shirts saying 'Babe'. I don't have girls, and, having been one myself ('But *why* can't I go out in the pelmet and the sequinned knickers? I am *fourteen*, you know'), I am sartorially very grateful. The following manage the miraculous feat of pleasing both me and my two sons – I am assuming they work with daughters too.

Mini Boden Surely I don't need to explain Mini Boden? A total lifesaver. For customer services and catalogue, call: 0845 357 5000, Mon–Sat, 8–8. Browse and buy online at www.boden.co.uk – though do beware, it's quite easy to go mad and spend zillions; e-mail: johnnie@boden.co.uk. They deliver worldwide. Baby Boden goes from 6 months, kids' stuff from 12 months to 14 years. I used to have real problems finding boys' pyjamas that didn't look like cotton shell suits and weren't exorbitant – Boden solved that. The clothes can take serious amounts of abuse, and last for ever, as far as I can see – they get handed down and down, and down again, and still look fine.

Semmalina 225 Ebury Street, London SW1W 8UT; tel: 020 7730 9333. Open: Mon–Sat, 9.30–5.30. Totally unhelpful if you don't live in London, as there isn't a catalogue or website – sorry. But this is as close as children get to their own version of über-boutiques like The Cross – it sells a fairly eclectic mixture of fairy dresses, funky T-shirts, jewellery (also for adults), raincoats, swords and Frisbees. It's a very cheering sort of shop, which is why I had to include it. Also, it's one of those shops that makes me quite furious that I don't have a girl.

Nippaz With Attitude Much as you'd expect from the name, i.e. high bling-bling content and a striking contrast with Semmalina (above). For customer services, call: 020 8769 0519, Mon–Fri, 9.30–5.30. Browse and buy online at www.nippaz.com; e-mail: info@nippaz.com. T-shirts from 0 to 6 years emblazoned with 'Milk, Milk, Lemonade', or Che Guevara, or 'Mama Ain't Raisin' No Fool'. My favourite is one that takes the AC/DC logo and changes it into BA/BY. Urban, shall we say: not for the admirer of the Peter Pan collar.

Little Badger Lovely knitwear for little creatures. For customer services and order line, call: 020 7620 2422, Mon–Fri, 9.30–5.30.

* You can buy from the entire range online at www.birkenstock.co.uk, handily.

Browse and buy online at www.littlebadger.com; also mail order – order your catalogue online or call customer services. They deliver worldwide. Knitwear goes from 0 to 8 years, cool T-shirts from 0 to 12. Think skull and crossbones jerseys, wool reindeer jackets, cotton ponchos, and things like *sweet* mice booties for babies. Good for presents. You can have your order sent in a pretty handmade gift box with a personal message – no Jiffy bags or bubble wrap here.

Green Baby 345 Upper Street, London N1 0PD; tel: 020 7359 7037. Open: Mon–Fri, 10–5; Sat, 10–6. Natural products and eco-friendly clothes and nappies – pure Islington, which isn't necessarily a commendation. If you're the kind of person who weaves her own sanitary towels, you'll be in heaven. Actually, I'm being facetious: even if you aren't, Green Baby is kind to the planet and kind to children's sensitive skin.* Browse and buy online at www.greenbaby.co.uk; worldwide delivery: now everywhere can be like Islington. Hooray (cough). For inquiries, call: 0870 240 6894, Mon–Fri, 9.30–5.30.

Little Shrimp 'Shorewear and seawear', they describe themselves as, which translates into lots of gorgeous stripiness – boat-neck tops, lovely candy-striped dresses, lovely candy-striped everything. From 3 months to 8 years. Browse online at www.littleshrimp.com; UK delivery. For mail order, call: 0845 602 3083, Mon–Fri, 10–5.

See also Gap Kids for the best, toughest denim, fleeces and chinos, though not for their seasonal ranges, which tend to feature unpleasant not-quite-right pastels and aren't as robust as the staples; M&S for school uniform – brilliant Teflon-coated trousers – underwear and the (very) odd pair of proper pyjamas; www.thekidswindow.com for those extremely sweet, durable, hickory-striped Osh Kosh B'Gosh children's dungarees that inexplicably seem to have disappeared from many bigger stores; and Asda for cheap, cheerful, longer-lasting than you'd expect everyday kicking-about-in clothes. Ching-ching (that's me patting my bottom, like AsdaMum in the ads. Lucky old AsdaMum – *her* children never wriggle around the trolley, faces smeared with chocolate, in the very vocal throes of a sugar rush).

* If you or your child has bad eczema, do visit Pure Cotton Comfort at www.eczemaclothing.com. They deliver worldwide. For inquiries and a catalogue call: 01524 730093; order lines are open 24 hours a day. They do kids' clothes, from organic nappies to school uniform via mitten pyjamas to stop scratching at night; also adults' tights, socks and underwear.

cosmetic) knowledge. God, those middle-class women. As though looking ugly made you Of The People. Anyway – I was shy and only just learning English, and so I didn't say anything, but it didn't stop me from thinking to myself that she had hands like raw hams and that a good blow-dry wouldn't have gone amiss, to say nothing of a slick of mascara and some decent lingerie. She needed The Shops, poor her, and she didn't know how. (At the time, the idea of anyone ingeniously making a political statement against patriarchy – we are wimmin and so on – simply by looking hideous didn't occur to me. I just felt sorry.)

There was a shop in Brussels called Dujardin, where all my *bon-chic-bon-genre* clothes came from: grey flannel pinafore dresses, pleated navy-blue woollen skirts, pastelly jerseys and heaps of that faux-Brit kit – duffle coats, kilts, tweedy things – that sends well-off Europeans into ecstasies (it still makes me smile – or wince in recognition – to see young French men of a certain kind wearing very neat jeans, brogues, a stripy shirt and a pale yellow cashmere jumper tied nonchalantly around their shoulders: *le style Anglais*, never seen *en Angleterre* ever. It's like upper-middle-class French children being called Kevin or Bryan: sweet, and not entirely uncomical).

Anyway, so there I was, in my clothes. For a while, in Brussels, I went to the local primary school, where I had a lovely time but was fairly acutely aware of my outfits, which were not like the clothes of other children. My best friend, Cécile, wore platform shoes, tiny broderie-anglaise tops with puffed sleeves, and miniskirts. She had long, wild-looking sort of hair; I had a chic crop (which would have been more chic had my ears not stuck out bonkersly and had I not looked like a boy – a young, curly-locked Greek shepherd boy, to be precise) and *the* most conservative, ankle-skimming, top-button-done-up wardrobe imaginable. But I was happy in my navy-blue cardigans and casual weekend corduroys, even though, thirty years later, I am sniggering to think of myself then.

Thrown into the mix was the fact that my mother kept running away to India and to Pakistan with me in tow. So in April there I'd be, Little Miss Square, and in May I'd be running around barefoot in a shalwaar kameez, bugging my grandmother to pierce my nose (which she eventually did, in the garden, with a red-hot sewing needle). And then we'd go back to Brussels — except once, when war broke out and we were stuck for several months; my grandmother showed me how to tie a sari and cook parathas as the bombs fell nearby, leaving huge craters (melodramatic, but true). Usually, though, it'd be a see-saw between the bliss of being hot in the sunshine in thin cotton clothing and the equal bliss (hmmm, kind of) of being cold in Belgium, swathed in itchy wool.

Having got my nose pierced by one grandmother — I snorted the earring-back by mistake and had to be held upside down, choking, until I coughed it up again, after which we let the hole close up — I thought I'd try my other granny for a few shopping expeditions. What I really wanted was a top with little puff sleeves like my friend Cécile. My mother, alas, had decided that such tops were tarty — and, looking back, Cécile didn't exactly exude wholesomeness, possibly because she had mini-bosoms. Of course, unwholesomeness is what you absolutely die for if you're a precocious child aware of her own squareness — and mini-bosoms too, ideally. So I set about persuading my grandmother. She had a house at the Belgian seaside, in a place called Le Zoute, and there, across from the promenade by the beach, was a shop called Princess, and in its window was a pale pink puff-sleeved top in fluffy angora. The shop itself was shockingly expensive, and patronized solely by small blonde girls who wore those coats with velvet collars in the winter. In the summers, at the beach, they wore designer bikinis and had lithe, elongated tennis-club limbs. There was something terrifying about those little girls — something arctic and Grace Kelly-like that was totally intimidating and used to make me feel as though I was a tinker just off the encampment. They

weren't mean or anything — one, Jessica, became my closest
summer-holidays friend for about ten years: we used to walk to
Holland together, along the beach, eat waffles at the café as soon
as we got there and race back, stuffed, to beat the tide. But the way
those girls looked — glacial and hot at the same time, like sexy Nazis
— really gave me the willies on the one hand, and made me sick with
jealousy on the other. Princess was where they all shopped.

    The shop was daunting. It had enormous windows, with very few
clothes on display: each 'piece' was shown as though it were a
priceless jewel. My grandmother balked at the price of the angora
jumper with puffy sleeves in the window, but I dragged her back
again and again to stare at it, until, eventually, we went in. I can't
remember if this was before or after the family firm, which made
wallpaper (and had once employed Magritte as a designer, oddly),
had gone bankrupt through the financial naiveté of my great-
grandfather's six daughters, but I think it must have been
afterwards, because my grandmother, her income suddenly slashed
and replaced by a certain temporary chippiness, didn't like being
there at all. This sort of shop had been her natural habitat, but she
couldn't really afford it any more. I was certainly aware of this, but
I really wanted the top with the puffy sleeves and so, manipulative
minx that I was, I pretended not to notice. The shop assistants were
snooty: my granny's fur coat had seen better days and I looked like a
brown boy with sticky-out ears and Greek hair. Buying the top was
not a comfortable experience — it made me want to pee with anxiety
— but I remember swanning out of the shop with my navy-and-white
Princess carrier bag (little crown above the 'i') feeling nothing short
of ecstatic. I wore that top until it quite literally fell apart. And so I
learned my first lesson about boutique shopping: it's scary, but only
the first time. And, observing my poor meek, smiling grandmother,
I decided that if shop assistants are going to be rude to you, and
you're not grand enough not to mind, the only course of action
that's going to make you feel better is to be rude back.

18

NOTABLY FRIENDLY SHOPS

Pickett (see page 104)

The L Boutique (see page 156)

Harper and Tom's (see page 130)

Melvyn at Australia Shopping Mall, for Ugg boots (see page 107)

Pashley Cycles (see page 51)

Puppy/Bedstock (see page 111)

Liz Earle (see page 80)

Cath Kidston (see page 112)

Meg Rivers (see page 48)

Viking office supplies (see page 128)

Les Senteurs (see page 86)

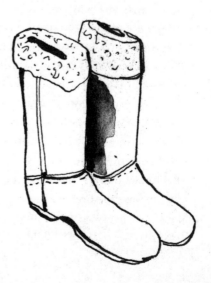

So there you go. Not a particularly edifying story, but then one's behaviour tends not to be particularly edifying in moments of extreme Shops anguish. A good shop assistant would have made my grandmother feel pleased to be in such an elegant shop, pleased to be parting with money she didn't have, pleased all round, really. (Obviously, a good child wouldn't have dragged her impecunious grandmother into such a shop in the first place. I *know*.) A really good shop assistant is like a soft mugger: he takes all your stuff, but very gently, cooing at you that your bag is divine, and then he gives you a quick metaphorical shoulder massage afterwards, so that you leave feeling displeased (no wallet left to speak of) but also strangely relaxed, strangely woozy and almost post-coital.

My mother is the rudest woman I know if shop assistants fail to please. Normally, of course, she is perfectly charming, and makes a point of being nice to them, especially if they are beautiful, or seem unhappy/poor, or are brunettes (we all have our prejudices). And she's been friends with the cashiers at her local branch of Sainsbury's for pretty much thirty years, greeting them all by name and having huge long chats. But if sales assistants are crap at their job and uninterested, or – God forbid – crap at their job, uninterested and *very glossy* (certain shops specialize in producing these, which I think is a mistake: you don't want your sales girl yawning and showing her expensive veneers while swathed in clouds of cashmere) . . . well, we're talking nuclear.

First, my mother raises an eyebrow – a particularly glacial eyebrow: its arc says, with stunning eloquence, 'You are just so unbelievably ghastly.' (I long to be able to do this with my eyebrow, but I just end up looking like I'm doing Roger Moore. Eyebrows matter almost more than anything else in your face, by the way: see box overleaf.)

WHERE TO GET YOUR BROWS DONE, AND WHY YOU SHOULD

You should because it's like having a mini face-lift. Seriously. Having perfect brows makes the most extraordinary difference to one's face: it opens everything up, makes you look perky, massively enhances the application of eye make-up, because you suddenly have acres of smooth brow to decorate, and – most crucially – makes you look properly pulled together and soignée in a way that nothing else can, even first thing in the morning. Who doesn't want to look chic first thing? Besides, if the eyes are the mirror of the soul, do you really want them to be badly framed, like bunging a Matisse in a frame from the pound shop? No, sisters, you do not. I would really not attempt to 'do' my own brows. When it's done properly, it's truly an art. When it's done badly – more often than not – it's an abomination, probably because the temptation to overpluck is irresistible. I have mine threaded, because my stupidly sensitive skin reacts to even the most expert plucking by coming out in welts and rashes. Threading is an amazingly dextrous procedure whereby the threader loops a length of cotton thread, holds one end around her finger and the other between her teeth, and catches tiny extraneous hair between the two pieces, neatly pulling it out by the root, one row at a time. It is extremely precise, almost painless and very quick. These are the threading queens in London:

- **Vashailly Patel**, who is the one I go to. Eyebrow threading and also utterly fabulous facials, including dermabrasion – having your face hoovered, basically. Salon: 51 Paddington Street, London W1U 4H. Open: Mon, 9–1, Tues–Sat, 9–6. For appointments and info, call: 020 7224 6088. Eyebrows: £30 for up to 15 minutes. NB: There's a waiting list.

- **Kamini Vaghela** at the Olympus Suite, Claridge's, Brook Street, London W1A 2JQ, Thurs, 10.30–3.30. For appointments, call: 020 7409 6565. £30 for up to 15 minutes. She is also at the Wyndham Place Beauty Clinic, 15 Wyndham Place, London W1H 2AQ, Mon, Wed, Fri, 10.30–6.30 (Wed, 7). For appointments, call: 020 7723 8838. £25 for up to 15 minutes.

- **Arezoo Kaviani**. Eyebrow threading, Brazilian waxes and variants thereon (don't ask), and very long (2–3 hours) facials. Private salon in the heart of Knightsbridge. Call Arezoo, who is lovely, on her mobile: 07768 903 090; no address given because she does so many celebs. She also applies crystal body jewellery, including on your front bottom – diamanté stars heading for the labia, that kind of thing. Eyebrows: £20–25 for up to 15 minutes.

- **Farida Choudhury** at Urban Retreat, Harrods, Mon, Tues, Wed, 9–7. For appointments, call: 020 7893 8333. £18 for up to 15 minutes.

Threading is long-lasting and just plain fabulous. If you don't have an eyebrow guru locally, this is one of the few things it's worth coming up to London for (do I sound mad? Try it. You'll thank me). But you may very well have a threader nearby. I live in a Turkish area, for instance, and some of the local salons do it if you ask (it's never advertised). If you have a local Asian or Middle Eastern community, it's worth inquiring, because someone somewhere is bound to be a champion threader. Speaking of which, do check the threader's name: I've never come across anyone with a non-Asian or non-Arab name who can do it properly. And never have your eyebrows waxed: it's almost impossible to do this with any real precision.

Being on the receiving end of the eyebrow is startling enough.
Hitherto bored, manicure-examining sales girls who have been
busy sneering at your shoes and thinking your bag is very last
season suddenly stand up straight, stare around them nervously
and get that look animals do when they know for a fact that a
bigger animal is going to eat them — the vole meets stoat look,
if you will. But it's too late! They should have paid attention
earlier! The stoat is heading in for the kill, and the vole, in one
horrible blinding moment of realization, knows it's her little
bones that are about to be snapped.

Post-eyebrow, we get an 'Excuse me?' so filled with disbelief
and contempt that, really, it sends shivers down the sturdiest
spines. When I was a teenager, out shopping with my mother,
this was the point at which I would endeavour to disappear. The
Excuse Me inevitably provokes stammering in the person to whom
it is addressed, and it is not comfortable to watch — nature red
in tooth and claw, and so on.

After the Excuse Me, and the gibbering, wet-palmed responses
it provokes, we get the attack proper, the vocabulary of which is
innocuous enough: 'Could you please explain to me why I have
been waiting for twenty minutes to find out if you have these in a
Medium/Waiting for you to stop chatting to your friend/Waiting
for service', etc. etc. The attack is delivered smoothly and softly —
the stoat, after all, dispatches its vole victim swiftly and does not
toy with it. The sales assistant is nearly in tears. My mother then
asks to speak to the manager.

My mother's intolerance in the face of bad service is founded
on two basic principles: a) that there is nothing wrong in working
in the service industry and b) that if a job's worth doing, it's worth
doing well. Having had a series of rubbish jobs for which I was
paid grotesquely small amounts of money, I can't entirely
concur, and so I can't do Vole–Stoat very well (there have been
exceptions). But a friend and I, having been treated like we were
two poos in frocks by an especially unlovely sales assistant in

Brompton Cross, once came up with an excellent, idiot-proof alternative. It's not Vole–Stoat, but it *is* pretty good. You stand there, feeling small and shabby and dissed, and then, as you're about to leave, you say to the (female) shop assistant, quite loudly,

YOU HAVE A MOUSTACHE.

You don't laugh: you are a compassionate fellow woman, offering advice. If you think you can manage it, you can wave your index finger around your upper lip a little, to illustrate, and make a little sad moue of sympathy. And then you leave.

Facial Hair and What to Do about It

*For God's sake, don't shave it. I know this sounds obvious, but
I also have two girlfriends who do just this and what started as a
drastic emergency measure before going out one night has now
turned into a hated daily ritual, performed through a haze of tears.
I really think there's something in the water, because practically
everybody I know has a story about going to bed looking perfectly
normal and waking up either with a 'tache or, creepily, with one
long stray hair in a particularly unlovely place, like the chin.
Obviously, these are to be tweezed out and absolutely nothing else.
As for the 'tache, I favour Jolene Cream Bleach,* but this only
works if you're not too hirsute, otherwise you just get a big Dutch-
looking blonde porn star 'tache instead of a dark, and arguably
more stylish, Frida Kahlo one. If you are indeed hirsute, get
yourself to the threader: if it's good enough for Asian and Arab
women with thick black hair, it's good enough for you. Failing this,
wax — if you can stand the pain and don't immediately acquire
social-life-destroying red welts on your upper lip for a week.
Electrolysis seems to me to be more trouble than it's worth. As
for Veet, formerly Immac, on the face . . . I don't think so.*

---

* From a chemist, as any fule kno.

I've completely digressed, though you'll thank me one day for the moustache tip. I was trying to ascertain whether there was such a thing as a shopping gene. This is kind of unlikely, I'll grant you — but I do believe that a love of shops is, as with so many other things, bred in the bone. If you think it's normal to go into ecstasies over sugar tongs, tennis shoes, crayons, book bindings, chess pieces and Bic cigarette lighters, and if all of your nearest and dearest agree, then those ecstasies become part of you, and part of your response to the world.

My father loved the shops too; mostly he loved buying motorbikes. I have a marvellous photograph of him taken in the South of France, under an avenue of lime trees, leggily straddling his giant bike, his black leathers matching his black hair. He must have been in his mid-forties. He is smiling up at the sky, as though to thank Our Lord for Kawasakis. In fact, he loved buying motorbikes so much that he packed in his job one day and opened a bike shop. I used to spend half of the school holidays with him in Brussels, and he'd have me model all the bike jackets — I especially remember a make called Furygan which had a snarling black panther on the back. He'd tell me all about the leather, the stitching, what kind of impact the leathers could withstand. (He was interested in this, having nearly lost a leg after a particularly nasty crash — two years in hospital and amputation only just averted by my twenty-something mother giving the doctors a daily dose of Vole–Stoat Ultra.) He loved his bike shop, he was truly happy; but having no experience of trade whatsoever, he died a double bankrupt, his prized Bennelli long gone to pay off creditors. His biker buddies, now old and bikeless, sent a wreath to his funeral.

So I know my bikes quite well. I also know my shirts. My father had dozens in pink, yellow and lavender; most of them came from England. They used to hang in his closet in blocks of colour, crisp and starched and immaculate, and sometimes I used to stare at them for ages, feeling utterly contented, feeling that order was a very good thing, and represented by these shirts.

He loved clothes, my dad, nearly as much as bikes, and he used to take me shopping in the holidays (pre-bankruptcy). He was one of those men who used to love, and appreciate, all the women around him — his wives, of whom there were many over the years, his daughter, his mother — to be well dressed. He was the opposite of mean: if you liked the Benetton skirt in pink, he'd buy it in red and in orange for you too. Being the kind of man he was, he had a horror of unfemininity, which, in my case, translated itself into the purchasing of clothes — at my urging — that my mother wouldn't necessarily have approved of: short clothes, or clothes with *décolletages*, or clothes that somehow felt racy (though perhaps only to me, since one of these was, bewilderingly in retrospect, an apple-green velour top with a giant collar and even more giant zip). I was, naturally, in heaven. The only thing wrong with his shopping skills was that he was unnaturally keen on yellow, my least favourite colour. There is a slew of photographs of me as a child looking jaundiced in yellow coats and yellow hats and yellow boots.

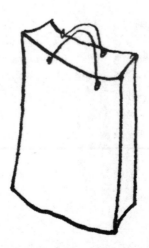

BEST SHIRTS FOR MEN

Gieves and Hawkes 1 Savile Row, London W1S 3JR; tel: 020 7434 2001. Open: Mon–Thurs, 9–6.30; Fri, 9–6; Sat, 10–6. Classic tailoring – you simply can't go wrong. Shops like this make me wonder why so many reasonably paid men are still badly dressed. Browse online at www.gievesandhawkes.com. Ready-to-wear from £59; bespoke from £165, which sounds quite grotesque until you've worn one. They make a brilliant birthday present for, say, your dad's sixtieth. The 'g' in Gieves is hard, as in 'give'.

Turnbull and Asser 71–72 Jermyn Street, London SW1Y 6PF; tel: 020 7808 3000. Open: Mon–Fri, 9–6; Sat, 9.30–6. For men and women. Make like James Bond and the Prince of Wales. Browse online at www.turnbullandasser.com. Ready-to-wear from £60; bespoke from £130 (but you need to order six). They take about twenty measurements and send you home to wash and dry the first shirt, adjusting the others accordingly if necessary. Amazing to think you can have a shirt constructed so that the cuffs work in harmony with the thickness of your watch.

New and Lingwood Ltd 53 Jermyn Street, London SW1Y 6 LX; tel: 020 7493 9621. Open: Mon–Fri, 9–6; Sat, 10–6. I know, I know, we're getting quite Sloaney here, but if you want the best, most classic, most stylish shirts, these four are where it's at. Browse and buy online at www.newandlingwood.com. Ready-to-wear from £75; bespoke from £140. Delightful service.

Richard James 29 Savile Row, London W1S 2EY; tel: 020 7434 0605. Open: Mon–Fri, 10–6 (Thurs, 7). Men's shirt heaven: every single one of these is simply utterly beautiful. Best described, rather naffly, as 'classic with a twist'. Exquisite colours, stripes, from £95. They do ready-to-wear and bespoke; their suits are to die for and adorn the best-dressed backs. Browse online at www.richardjames.co.uk. If you like something (and you will), call the shop and they'll send it to you. They deliver worldwide. Also – not to be sniffed at – everyone at the shop is lovely, from Mr James down.

When I last saw my father, in an old people's home in the
Ardennes, he was dying of cancer and Alzheimer's. He was
extremely badly dressed, in a horrible sweatshirt and floppy
trousers — and the adult nappy had never been part of his
repertoire before. He was completely gaga. I went outside and
smoked twenty cigarettes and sobbed away to myself, and then
I gave the nurse money to buy him decent clothes that fitted him.
She said that his clothes were freshly laundered every day and that
he didn't mind what he wore. I did Vole–Stoat: my mother's
daughter, as well as my pink-and-lavender-shirted father's.
When he died and I collected his things, there were two crisp
new shirts, a new navy cardigan and two new pairs of brown cords
in his wardrobe. And on his dressing table, there was a picture
of me peering out grumpily in a canary-yellow anorak.

Big Fat Dinners

Even those of us — those of you, rather — who absolutely loathe shopping can't get away from the fact that we all have to do it. And nowhere is this more evident than in the question of food shopping: what we want to eat, what we want to feed our loved ones, how we see food, how much effort we're prepared to make for it . . . All of these are questions that we address, or choose not to address by peering gloomily into the fridge and wailing that there's nothing to eat, on a daily basis.

I find the idea of venturing forth to market with my little shopping basket of a morning quite extraordinarily alluring. If you read food writers as devotedly as I do, you too will have been encouraged to go to the shops with no preconceived ideas and to buy what looks good and fresh and enticing that day. This is, naturally, admirable advice. But my goodness, it's hard to live up to. First, it presupposes that you have the kind of charming local high street-cum-Provençal market town — ruddy-cheeked baker, organic butcher, fruit and veg man who stocks courgette flowers, olive shop — that sadly more closely resembles some fevered foodie fantasy than the reality in OOs Britain: I have Dixie Fried Chicken and three separate pound shops. Secondly, who has the time? I'm happy to spend the odd Saturday morning traipsing from fabulous cheese shop to extravagant *pâtisserie* to, yes, organic butcher's, but it isn't a journey I have the time, money or inclination to undertake every day.

Happily — and the happiness in question is of the quasi-delirious kind — an amazing amount of what we might rather naffly term 'gourmet' shopping can now be done online. You can get really terrific organic meat delivered; prosciutto from Italy, plus home-made pesto and the best aged Parmesan; moist, dense, convincingly as-made-by-granny cakes; rose-petal jelly; genuine

Turkish delight, translucent and studded with pistachios; really
good, taste-the-difference organic flour for your bread machine
(Panasonic is the one you're after — they only make one kind.
Don't even think of getting another sort — the Panasonic is
absolutely worth the extra cash). I get *delicious* kippers sent
overnight by registered post from the Isle of Bute. Oh, and wine —
rivers of (not from the Isle of Bute). Is it expensive? Well, yes,
an organic chicken costs more than some revolting abortion of
a battery number, but you knew that anyway. Personally, I'd rather
eat better meat less often. You pay postage and packing, of course,
but then you'd pay petrol and parking, or congestion charge,
or bus fare or minicab fare to go shopping anyway.

And the beauty of this is that you shop when you feel like it: when
the children are finally asleep, or at six in the morning, or while on
the phone to someone exceptionally dull (trying to click your mouse
quietly, and failing: 'What's that noise?' 'The radiators.') And
it's quick. I'd have hesitated to recommend these shops quite so
enthusiastically a couple of years ago, because online ordering was
still in its infancy, but it's now bang up to date and ultra efficient.
You can't go wrong, and there is something enormously pleasing
about not traipsing out to Tesco when it's cold and rainy and you
just know the stir-crazy children are raring to go mad in the aisles.

ONLINE SUPERMARKETS EXPLAINED

There is no doubt that these are a lifesaver, especially if you live somewhere remote and don't drive. In addition, they're usually a safe bet for the odd 'exotic' ingredient, if your village shop doesn't stock, say, fresh lime leaves. And there's no denying that having your mineral water delivered – though see also the excellent, cheaper-in-the-long-run under-sink water purification system described below* – is nicer than humping great crates of it about. BUT in my experience, successful home deliveries depend entirely on wherever supermarket X's warehouse is, how well said warehouse is stocked and how scrupulous the person putting together your order is. My London branch of Tesco is utterly feeble: they routinely fail to deliver the most basic staples, such as spaghetti or Cheddar, and replace other stuff with things I would never consider eating: organic eggs replaced with economy battery eggs, for example. Worse, anything fresh that I might order from them – a chicken, the last time – arrives unchilled and within twenty-four hours of its use-by date. Basically, they're hopeless. I am currently renting a house in the country, where it's a different story. My order arrives with no missing items, the driver is charming, the substitutions are intelligent and the whole experience is both pleasing and effortless. Given that standards vary so widely depending on location, there's nothing for it but to try them all out and see which one works best for you. My own favourites are the impeccable, reliable, helpful Ocado, who deliver in partnership with Waitrose in London; and Tesco in the country. But out of all the supermarkets, Ocado wins hands down for all-round friendliness (I'm making them sound like Babarpapa).

Sainsbury's www.sainsburystoyou.com
Customer care: 0845 301 2020
Opening hours: Mon–Sat, 8–10.30; Sun, 10–6

Tesco www.tesco.com
Customer services: 0800 505 555, Mon–Sat, 9–6

Waitrose www.waitrosedeliver.com
Customer services: 0800 188 884

Ocado www.ocado.com
Customer care: 0845 399 1122 (unusually, they have one-hour delivery slots, which is pretty damned useful if you're in a hurry)

---

* The Fresh Water Filter Company Ltd design, manufacture and fit water-purification equipment. The FW 1000 Drinking Purifier fits neatly under the sink and provides endless clean drinking water. It's great, and somehow seeing it there makes you drink more water, and thus have better skin. Browse and buy online at www.freshwaterfilter.com, or call: 020 8597 3223.

These are a godsend. I don't eat meat that often, and when I do, I want it to be *fantastic*, and as free of rubbish as is humanly possible. The nearest good butcher to me is some distance away – it used to take me two hours there and back to go and buy steak. Not any more. The three companies below come especially highly recommended.

Donald Russell Terrific organic meat. Based in Aberdeenshire. Browse and buy online at www.donaldrussell.co.uk. They will deliver to the UK mainland; call them to see about delivery elsewhere: 01467 629666, Mon–Fri, 9–5; Sat, 9–1.

Swaddles Green Farm Organic meat, home-produced ready meals (if you must – these are pretty good) and children's meals (good burgers and exceptional bangers). Browse and buy online at www.swaddles.co.uk. Tel: 01460 234387, Mon–Fri, 9–4. Oddly, they also do an extremely delicious Christmas cake.

Eastbrook Farms Top-class organic meat; amazingly good chickens (but so's everything else). Browse and buy online at www.helenbrowningorganics.co.uk. They deliver nationwide; for inquiries, call: 01793 790460.

Staples are easy enough to come by via your supermarket, either in person or online. Delis are a different kettle of fish. Most towns have one, and it's often not very good. So many del is are a complete swizz: they stick some mediocre, manky olives into a load of vaguely Provençal bowls, whiz up some old fish and cream and call it *mousse de poisson*, have badly refrigerated displays of ancient sausages and dusty packets of overpriced biscuits — and you're supposed to swoon with admiration and delight, lick your chops and loosen your purse strings on the spot. I don't think so. I've noticed these kinds of delis are especially prominent in areas that are 'up and coming'. It's a crafty ploy: the middle-class residents of some formerly working-class bastion shriek with excitement, thinking the deli means the area has finally 'arrived', and so patronize the shop faithfully, even though it's rubbish; the deli stays open; everyone's happy (except people with taste buds or sense). Sooner or later, along comes Starbucks. Tara and Adrian are delirious; the nice little caff that did great breakfasts goes under. And now I am depressing myself. What I was trying to say is that good delis are actually few and far between. Cherish yours if you have one, and if not, buy online.

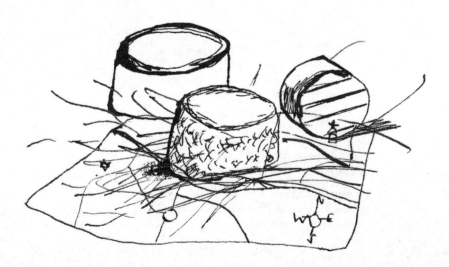

Valvona & Crolla 19 Elm Row, Edinburgh EH7 4AA; tel: 0131 556 6066. Open: Mon–Sat, 8–6.30. Fabulous, fabulous deli and wine merchants. The man who founded this *walked* to Scotland from Tuscany. Browse and buy online at www.valvonacrolla-online.co.uk; they can send orders out the same day. Will ship (non-perishables) worldwide. There's also a yummy café.

Esperya Fabulous also. More than one London restaurant I know relies on their amazing hams and aged Parmesans. Chianina beef from Tuscany (*nec plus ultra*) sent out every Tuesday. Home-made pesto of great deliciousness. Dozens of meats, cheeses, wines, olive oils, coffees, sweeties, and the best plum tomatoes and preserved vegetables. Browse and buy online at www.esperya.com/english within the EU. For orders and delivery elsewhere, plus inquiries, e-mail: info@esperya.com.

Paxton & Whitfield 93 Jermyn Street, London SW1Y 6JE; tel: 020 7930 0259. Open: Mon–Sat, 9.30–6. Cheesemongers that don't need an introduction; also 'gourmet food'. They also provide marvellous gift packs: e.g. Teatime Quintet Box – lemon curd, fruit cake, strawberry jam, afternoon tea caddy, oatcakes – £20; or Ploughman's Box – wooden box with pound of Cheddar, pheasant pâté, real ale, biscuits for cheese and chutney – £26. Browse and buy online at www.paxtonandwhitfield.co.uk. They can deliver worldwide, although call the mail-order number to be advised: 01608 650660.

La Fromagerie 30 Highbury Park, London N5 2AA; tel: 020 7359 7440. Open: Mon, 10.30–7.30; Tues–Fri, 9.30–7.30; Sat, 9.30–7; Sun, 10–5. The utter bee's knees of cheese palaces. Also sweetmeats, Poilane bread, olives, cakes, pastries, etc. etc. Browse online at www.lafromagerie.co.uk, then call them. They can deliver the unperishable goods worldwide. Also at: 2–4 Moxon Street, London W1U 4EW; tel: 020 7935 0341. Open: Mon, 10.30–7.30; Tues–Fri, 8.30–7.30; Sat, 9–7; Sun, 10–5. There is a 'tasting café' at the back of this shop – drop in and FEAST on wine and cheese. They also have a wonderful dinner party service within London: they'll cook you homy, delicious food, recommend and bring cheeses, wines and so on.

In my experience, Waitrose has by far the best deli counter of any high-street supermarket; the best deli 'dry goods' too, including jars of Dean & Deluca pasta sauce, which really are the ant's pants.

Now, to drink. Buying wine is fun if you can taste it, but not so much fun, in my opinion, if you're in a hurry down your local offy, staring at the Lambrusco and the Bull's Blood (actually not at all bad, but you get my point). Buying it sight unseen online may seem odd, but the sites below are excellent. Berry Bros, in particular, keep a note of your past purchases and suggest similar things you might like — these haven't failed me yet. Their house wines are fantastic for everyday drinking: I am sipping Berry Bros Good Ordinary Claret, £4.95 a bottle, as I write (true). Soon I may go for a little nap. Terrible thing, afternoon drinking.

WINE ONLINE

Everywine.co.uk Virtually every wine online. Buy same-wine cases at www.everywine.co.uk. They deliver to mainland UK; call customer services to be advised for any offshore areas: 0800 072 0011.

Also sister company, www.booths-wine.co.uk. This site allows you to choose your own mixture of any twelve bottles of wine by colour/style, price, country or grape. They have also chosen their best wines and put them together in pre-mixed cases. They deliver to mainland UK; call customer services to be advised about any other areas and for inquiries: 0800 197 0066.

Berry Bros & Rudd 3 St James's Street, London SW1A 1EG; tel: 020 7396 9600. Open: Mon–Fri, 10–6; Sat, 10–4. Wonderful, helpful website, with excellent follow-through customer services – inspirational and very friendly (you don't need to be a wine boffin or spend a lot of money). Really informative, too – you come away from the site feeling you've learned something. Browse and buy online at www.bbr.com. They can deliver worldwide; call to be advised: 0870 900 4300.

It's beginning to sound like Waitrose sponsor me, but never mind: they definitely have the best wine aisles of the supermarkets.

The companies I've picked out ship nationally, and in many cases internationally (though not fresh meat or fish, obviously). If you set up a regular order, the better ones will ship to a holiday address – even somewhere quite remote – for two weeks in July, or whatever, so that you're not suddenly at the mercy of Meatland or Greggs the Baker.* Having said that, Greggs the Baker does oddly good sausage rolls in an emergency, even though it probably wouldn't do to dwell too deeply over their contents.

 * Organic box schemes do this too. My favourite is the Fresh Food Company – www.freshfood.co.uk. Not just fruit and veg either, but staples too.

IF YOU CAN'T BE ARSED TO COOK
BUT SHUN THE MICROWAVE

Leaping Salmon Home-delivered food kits – totally great.
You browse their menu (which changes frequently) online at
www.leapingsalmon.com, decide what you want – one course,
three, wine too, different puddings – and order. Next-day delivery
nationwide; same-day in central London (check website for list
of postcodes) if you order before 5 p.m. Mon–Fri and 3.30 p.m. on
Sat. For inquiries or to order, call: 0870 701 9100. Also kiosks at
Paddington and Victoria stations, among others. What is
remarkable about Leaping Salmon is that the food they send out –
part-assembled, with instructions – actually tastes good and, dare
one say it, home-made. If I really couldn't cook – well, if I really
couldn't cook, I'd learn, but if I were, say, an inept bloke trying to
make a romantic dinner for two, this is where I'd come to. And then
I'd hurry along to Amazon, to buy Nigella. Not knowing how to cook
because you're a bloke is *pathetic*. Please learn.

The Grocer on Elgin 6 Elgin Crescent, London W11 2HX; tel:
020 7221 3844. Really fabulous ready-made food to take home or have
delivered nationwide, from one of the co-founders of the Sugar Club
restaurant. Seriously yummy, though not cheap: think of it as having
restaurant-quality food in the comfort of your own home rather than
as an upmarket takeaway. At the time of writing, the menu included
fragrant Thai-inspired soups, delicious, thyme-rich (cash poor,
ho ho) beef stew, four different kinds of mash, pistachio meringues
that look like works of art, and so on. Robust, but sexy, if you like.
Call for information, or see www.thegroceron.com, from which
you can also order directly.

See also **Swaddles**, page 35 – their ready meals are in a different
league from the usual. In the high street – I used to test ready meals
for the *Sunday Times* years ago – Waitrose and M&S are the least
revolting.

I am fanatically interested in food and have been since infancy.
When I was small, in Brussels, my favourite food used to be
marrow-bones scraped out on to toast, closely followed by steak
tartare, or *filet americain* as it's known elsewhere, with thin chips
(I love England, but what's with the crazy fat, flooby chips?).

I don't know where my devotion to raw meat or bone marrow
came from, but it still exists, and nothing irritates me as much
as the yucks of faux-coy disgust these affiliations still occasionally
elicit from people who routinely eat pig snout 'n' scrotum – and
eyeball – in their cheap sausages. The greater part of the reason
for my irritation is that, to me, these foods taste of home (though,
oddly enough, I don't make a point of thinking of Brussels as
'home' ordinarily), and criticizing the foods feels rather like
being criticized myself. It's that old thing: you can say, 'My brother
is barking mad,' but if anyone has the temerity to agree, you want
to beat them up. Same with food. And food, surely, is all about
comfort – not the 'I fancy a carb overdose' comfort-eating that
comes post-hangover, but rather the idea of eating your way home.

HANGOVER CURES

You have two options, as far as I am aware, with a prairie oyster as a very butch potential third (ingredients: olive oil, an egg yolk, 1 tsp ketchup, a dash of Worcestershire sauce and/or Tabasco, salt and pepper. Swirl olive oil around the glass, then discard. Add rest of ingredients – don't break the yolk – and down in one). If you can stomach this, you can probably stomach Fernet Branca, the herby liqueur, which works very well but is, shall we say, an acquired taste, particularly if you're feeling delicate. My favoured option is D. R. Harris's Original Pick-me-up, a miraculous potion from the (lovely) chemist's of the same name at 29 St James's Street, London SW1A 1HB; tel: 020 7930 3915. Open: Mon–Fri, 8.30–6; Sat, 9.30–5. Buy online at www.drharris.co.uk – they ship worldwide. If you should be sauntering around St James's, Bertie Wooster-like, and feeling a bit peaky, you could go into the shop and have a shot of the Pick-me-up there and then (you might, while you're at it, buy some almond shaving soap; notice that all the packaging is beautiful, and make a mental note to come back whenever you're looking for Dad-style presents).

Naturally, all of the above remedies are improved beyond measure if combined with bed, telly and tea.* The tea really should be Barry's Tea, red label – the best builder's tea in the world, which for some inexplicable reason is only on sale in Ireland (where it's made) and the US. You can also sometimes find it in the odd supermarket in Irish areas. Why isn't it everywhere? It seems mad to me, with such a delicious product. Anyway, if you see it, stock up. Barry's is fantastic. Though do be warned – everything changes after your first cup and you can never go back.

---

* If you're a (rich) hungover man and in London, you could try the Refinery, an excellent men-only spa whose treatments include Hair of the Dog – aromatherapy, enzymatic mud wrap, facial detox; lasts 3 hours and costs £170. They claim no hangover will survive this onslaught. Buy gift tokens online at www.the-refinery.com or visit either 60 Brook Street, Mayfair, London WIK 5DU; tel: 020 7409 2001 (open 7 days a week), or 38 Bishopsgate, London EC2N 4AJ; tel: 020 7588 1006 (open Mon–Fri). They don't just do expensive packages, obviously; you can just as easily go in for a manicure or a wet shave – or indeed a buttock wax – but book first. The tokens make good presents.

My entire family is greedy. I wish greed weren't considered such
an appalling thing to confess to: I know people who claim to have
eating disorders instead of 'fessing up to being greedy and without
self-control. People eat in very different ways, it seems to me, and
one of the ways of eating is To Excess. Really, so what? My mother
is very greedy, for instance, but has self-discipline: if she eats too
much on Monday, she'll make a point of eating less on Tuesday.
I'd say this was admirably normal. One of my sisters is very greedy,
but doesn't like getting fat: if she eats a lot on Monday, she will,
mildly more dramatically, eat only fruit on Tuesday. Again, I
don't see how this is odd. I am very, *very* greedy, and if I eat too
much on Monday, I may wake up starving on Tuesday and may
very well make myself eggs Benedict for breakfast. This is because
my self-discipline is not all it might be. If I get fat, I'm either
annoyed enough to do something about it or I'm content to
think, My trousers are digging in a bit, but yumorama, that
dinner was delicious – the latter option being an unattractive
form of arrogance, I expect.

Having watched greedy people make excuses for their actions –
eating disorders, thyroids, mysterious stomach complaints – I'd
say quite a lot of us are too embarrassed to admit to anything as
basic, as boring, as unsexy as rampant greed for big fat dinners.
Odd, isn't it? These days, many of us feel more comfortable
having group therapy – standing in a room full of strangers,
weeping and lobbing accusations at everyone (except ourselves) –
than we would saying anything as pedestrian as, 'I am incredibly
greedy and I have no self-control, it's a total bummer.' We have to
have An Illness instead. It's very twenty-first century. *Quel* crock –
and sorry, but I'm not wasting a chapter on shopping for a new
head. Call me old-fashioned, but I'd rather shop for shoes.

HATE YOUR HEAD?
TRY THESE GREAT WIGS

Trendco Hair Centre are specialists in wigs and hair accessories (this is where you come and get the hairpiece for your twenty-first/fortieth/wedding). You can browse their vast range online at www.wigsattrendco.co.uk. and there is also a good catalogue available. London salon: 229 Kensington Church Street, London W8 7LX; tel 020 7221 2646. Open: Mon–Sat, 10–6 (last appointment with a consultant at 5). Walk-in appointments are available but those who have booked will be seen first. Clients are allocated a stylist and taken into a private room to try on different styles of wig. Wigs and hairpieces are from £59. As well as specially made wigs, there are ready to wear wigs in up to 27 colours. An imaging consultation is available, £25 for 20 minutes (redeemable if you purchase a wig), for those who want to change their image or colour their hair and want to know what they would look like before they take the plunge. The place is also a godsend if you've had chemo. Children's range, too. Staff are very helpful.

TOO FAT? DETOX AT THESE (BEST LONDON SPAS)

Bliss World Spa for men and women (no showering facilities for men). Browse online for spa treatments at www.blissworld.com. American and UK site. To book, call: 020 7584 3888; lines are open 24 hours a day. Bliss London: 60 Sloane Avenue, London SW3 3DD. Open: Mon–Fri, 9.30–8 (Wed, alternate weeks, 12.30); Sat, 9.30–6.30; Sun, 12–6. You need to book 3–5 weeks in advance for weekends and evenings, and 2–3 days for daytime appointments. The Deep Sea Detox slims, remineralizes, relaxes and hydrates. £120 for 90 minutes.

Mandarin Oriental Spa Most luxe in London, for men and women. Browse treatments online at www.mandarinoriental.com. For Mandarin London Spa inquiries and bookings, call: 020 7838 9888. Spa, Mandarin Oriental Hyde Park Hotel, 66 Knightsbridge, London SW1X 7LA. Open: 7 days a week, 7–10. You need to book 1–2 weeks in advance for weekdays, 4–6 weeks for weekends. The therapists create a tailor-made experience for £85 an hour, minimum 2 hours.

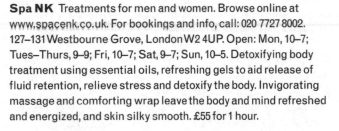

Spa NK Treatments for men and women. Browse online at www.spacenk.co.uk. For bookings and info, call: 020 7727 8002. 127–131 Westbourne Grove, London W2 4UP. Open: Mon, 10–7; Tues–Thurs, 9–9; Fri, 10–7; Sat, 9–7; Sun, 10–5. Detoxifying body treatment using essential oils, refreshing gels to aid release of fluid retention, relieve stress and detoxify the body. Invigorating massage and comforting wrap leave the body and mind refreshed and energized, and skin silky smooth. £55 for 1 hour.

I really think it's such a pity that a delight in food should be seen by some as a problem, or indicative of 'issues', or even as an illness. I mention it because I resent, I suppose, the idea that our family's absolute love of food should be seen by anybody as peculiar or wrong, when I consider it to be absolutely joyous, generous, nurturing, celebratory, and all those other words you might find used about food in a magical realism novel (remember them?) involving recipes.

FIVE FABULOUS BOOKS ABOUT LOVING YOUR DINNERS

- **Kitchen Essays** by Agnes Jekyll, Persephone Books (oh, the bliss of Persephone Books! See www.persephonebooks.co.uk for the full range, and buy online for £10 each). Collected articles from *The Times*, written in the 1920s with the then radical assumption that one didn't necessarily have armies of staff. Chapters – beautifully written, sparkling, witty and knowing – are called things like 'A Little Supper after the Play', 'Food for Artists and Speakers' and 'For the Too Thin'. An absolute delight to read – a lesson on how to write, in parts – and the recipes have held up surprisingly well.

- **The Constance Spry Cookery Book**. (Out of print, unbelievably.*) Much better than Mrs Beeton, but same sort of matronly, comforting, no-nonsense gist. When my mother and I first moved to London, we used to have a lovely downstairs neighbour called Ian, who, improbably, made his own croissants and was the most amazing cook. I used to hang around in his flat, drooling and trying to help, and on my twelfth (I think) birthday, he gave me this book. It tells you everything from how to bone a chicken to what to feed invalids and has the best ever recipe for the retro delight that is Coronation Chicken. Actually, it has recipes for everything in the whole world – dozens of ways with potatoes, how to make every single sauce you've ever heard of, heavenly, very English puddings (excellent section on offal, too). Old-fashioned but totally useful, and a welcome antidote to glossy books with too many pictures by celebrity chefs.

- **Cooking in Ten Minutes** by Edouard de Pomiane (Serif, £5.99). Written in 1948 – and he really means it about the ten minutes. Like being instructed by a very charming, rather sexy, slightly louche rogue uncle – i.e. heaven to read. The recipes work brilliantly and taste good – at least the handful I've tried did – if you can overcome your twenty-first-century distaste at the unapologetic plainness of the ingredients (he likes tins). But whether you use this to cook from or just to read, it's a classic. Every home should have one – and it's a lifesaver if you're hard-up.

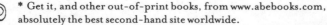

 * Get it, and other out-of-print books, from www.abebooks.com, absolutely the best second-hand site worldwide.

- **Arabella Boxer's Book of English Food**. (Out of print,
  though for heaven's sake, couldn't somebody please republish?)
  Boxer was the *Sunday Times*'s food writer, and *Vogue*'s. This book
  is about English food in the 1920s and 1930s – part history, part
  cookery book, setting the dishes in their social and economic
  context and reprinting recipes from magazines of the time,
  from nursery food to dinner party dishes. Wonderful to read.

- **Much Depends on Dinner** by Margaret Visser. (Out of print too.
  How can this be?) Absolutely gripping treatise on how we eat –
  full of research, lightly worn, and bizarre, compelling historical
  detail. A total page-turner, and more elegantly written than
  many novels.

Food, I think, is all to do with home: whether we suffer from
a desire to run back towards it or to run away from it, the two are
intrinsically linked. My maternal grandmother used to rustle up
the most amazing breakfast of parathas (sometimes stuffed with
potato) and chilli-hot eggs, speckled with coriander. My sisters
and I were all brought up on these – not every day, because then
we'd weigh thirty stone and have to be craned out of bed, but every
now and then, as the treat to end all treats. To this day, they are
our favourite breakfast, now made by our mother for special
occasions, like birthdays. Just as the new vegetarian might feel
longing pangs at the smell of bacon sizzling, so we abandon
any dietish urges at the very idea of – swoonorama – a stuffed
paratha, the king of breads.

BREAD AND CAKES

Meg Rivers Utterly delicious cakes and caky gifts by post. You can buy online at www.megrivers.com. Delivery to UK mainland only; for other destinations and inquiries, call: 01608 682858. All products are suitable for vegetarians and can be frozen, with the exception of iced cakes – which means you need never be cakeless again! You can stuff the freezer with gingerbread and award-winning brownies and cherry cake! They also have a yummy, non-sandally wheat-free range. They do excellent gift packs: lovely ready-made tuck boxes, for instance, or the Starving Student Box, which would make your undergraduate son, living on spaghetti hoops and plastic toast, really love you.

The Bread Shop 17 Brewer Street, London W1 0RJ; tel: 020 7434 3408. Open: Mon–Wed, 8–7.30; Thurs–Sat, 8–11. Delicious organic bread and also, more unusually, delicious wheat-free croissants and loaves that don't taste like papier mâché. You can browse online at www.thebreadshop.com. Also at: 65 St John's Wood High Street, London NW8 7NL; tel: 020 7586 5311. Open: Mon–Fri, 7–6.30; Sat, 7–6; Sun, 8–5. You can place an order by phone and pick up at your convenience.

Flourbin.co.uk Very wide and exotic range of top-quality, gunk-free flours for baking and bread machines; also nuts, seeds, yeasts. Use these and you'll never use supermarket flour again – and think how smug you'll feel (I know I do) when making the children's packed lunches, knowing the bread is home-made and bursting with utter goodness.

Buxtonfoods.com This is like an online health-food shop; it stocks Terence Stamp's wheat-free breads. Giving up wheat, when you've spent your time sneering at people with so-called food allergies or intolerances, is quite telling. Basically, you shrink dramatically. If you can't get to the Bread Shop (above), Stamp's is the only wheat-free bread worth eating, but do keep it in the fridge, otherwise it goes off almost instantly. Sainsbury's now also has a broad and excellent range of wheat-free pastas, biscuits, cakes and so on, called Free From.

The vast majority of my childhood memories *en Belgique* are food-related. When we were staying at my granny's at the seaside, for six weeks every summer, I'd get up in the morning and cycle to the baker's to get the breakfast *petits pains*, still warm from the oven, to be devoured with either quince jelly (oh, God, quince jelly — I could write poems) or the tiny little shrimp known as *crevettes grises*. You hollowed out the little crusty rolls and stuffed the hollow with curls of unsalted butter and the shrimp: as a start to the day, it's never been bettered. I remember the bicycle ride, the sheer exhilarating pleasure of being on my own, aged ten or eleven, pedalling past the villas with neat gardens and weathervanes,* sniffing the salty air which made my hair sticky, knowing that after breakfast we would go to the beach. Despite having spent my teenagehood thinking of myself as some sizzling-hot Latina type — there weren't then many role models for mixed-race girls, and you grab what you can — I now realize, in my late thirties, that I am exactly what I am, which is to say I am a person who can reduce herself to tears by looking out at the flat grey North Sea (or by listening to Jacques Brel singing of the same). I wish I were a Californian beach bunny, ready to party in a glittery pink bikini and heels, but I'm not: I like shrimps and low sky and purple-black mussels clinging to the grey rocks.

* Weathervanes! Have a look at the utterly poetic loveliness on offer from Otter Wrought Iron Products at www.weathervanes.co.uk; tel 01787 475060 — they'd make poetically lovely presents too.

QUINCES

BUY YOUR QUINCE TREE FROM HERE

Keepers Nursery sells quince and other fruit and nut trees. You can buy online at www.keepers-nursery.co.uk; for inquiries or a catalogue, call: 01622 726465. Trees are supplied between mid-November and mid-March. Quince-wise, they recommend the Meeches Prolific, as it crops very well, and supply 1–3-year-old trees. Keepers are remarkably helpful, and a quince tree makes a lovely present for somebody.

HOW TO MAKE QUINCE JELLY

Makes 1.8–2.25 kg (4–5 lb)
1.8 kg (4 lb) quinces
2 lemons
sugar

Wash and roughly chop the quinces. Put them in a heavy-bottomed pan with just enough water to cover. Bring to the boil and simmer, covered, for about 1$^{1}/_{2}$ hours, or until very soft. Strain through a muslin cloth. This takes ages – like a couple of hours – because if you squeeze and push and get impatient, the mixture goes cloudy. Measure the volume of the liquid, then add 450g (1 lb) of sugar for each 600 ml (1 pint) of liquid. Place the juice back into a heavy-bottomed saucepan, add the sugar, stir until fully dissolved and bring to the boil. Cook rapidly for 10–15 minutes until the setting point is reached. Skim and pot.

WHERE TO GET LOVELY BIKES

I like old-fashioned bikes, the kind that glide along in a stately manner, allowing you to take in your environs, as opposed to whizzy ultra-light, ultra-speedy, good-for-commuter numbers. Both the bikes below are really heavy, really beautiful, and have extremely well-upholstered and comfy leather saddles. You know, presumably, where to get their cool, semi-professional aluminium-framed counterparts (complete with Saddle of Pain); I offer these two as a charming, but not necessarily time-efficient alternative. They're the kind of bikes you might use to ride to the baker's to buy your morning buns, not to cross London at rush hour on. Though I suppose you could, if you had strong calves – I used to cycle from Elephant and Castle to Soho on my Pashley years ago, when I was fit.

Pashley Cycles Lovely, beautiful hand-built bikes that make you feel like cycling through rustic villages and fields of wheat with roses in your hair. The absolute opposite of those light, speedy, futuristic-looking numbers, and all the better for it – these are the kinds of bike Miss Marple would ride (and have brainwaves on). You can browse online at www.pashley.co.uk. They can deliver worldwide either themselves or through one of their distributors; phone to be advised. For info, help and orders, call: 01789 292263, Mon–Fri, 8.30–5. Adult bikes range from £300. Also good selection for those with special needs – and the people at Pashley are extremely friendly.

Electra Bicycle Company Again, lovely old-fashioned-looking 'cruiser' bikes with squidgy, comfy saddles – marginally edgier than the Pashleys, in that they recall 1950s America rather than 1920s England. You can browse online at www.electrabike.co.uk (or .com for the US); dealers are listed on the site. Check out the Ladies Hawaii 3 in turquoise or pink, £289, with painted-on little white flowers: a thing of beauty and a joy for ever.

SEAFOOD SUPPLIERS

Ritchie's of Rothesay 111 Montague Street, Rothesay, Isle of Bute, Scotland. Open: Mon–Sat, 7–5. Non-dyed kippers traditionally smoked over oak (which are broken-down oak whisky casks) on their own premises. Call: 01700 505414, also for details of their forthcoming website. EU delivery. They also sell smoked salmon and trout. All products are available throughout the year.

Martin's Sea-Fresh Fish Direct from Cornwall. Browse and buy online at www.martins-seafresh.co.uk or call: 0800 027 2066. Fresh and smoked fish are delivered overnight; also shellfish.

The Fish Society Frozen, not fresh. Browse and buy online at www.thefishsociety.co.uk. They will deliver 200 different sorts of fish to your door, including sushi portions.

FARM SHOPS

Farm shops, and the local produce they supply, are my new favourite thing. This shop, housed in an old barn, is owned by Katharine Assheton, an old schoolfriend (and a raving beauty – which I mention because I do think it helps, if you're out buying eggs, to be served by Helen of Troy). Longborough is attached to a fruit farm of the same name, and is a model of how farm shops should be: airy, friendly and magnificently well stocked. You can buy the farm's fruit frozen, by the scoop; fantastic local meat; excellent cheese and dairy products; locally made ready meals; and the best Summer Pudding for miles. The shops stocks brilliant staples too, and you can even have a coffee when you've finished shopping – how civilized is that? Plants and herbs are sold in the garden (where there's a climbing frame). Check the website for updates and events. Longborough Farm Shop, Longborough, Moreton-in-Marsh, Gloucestershire GL56 0QZ; tel: 01451 830469; fruit-pickers' hotline: 01451 830413. Open: Mon–Sat, 9–6; Sun, 10–6; www.longboroughfarmshop.com.

I only have one bad food memory: trying the unspeakable fizzy drink Dr Pepper. It was Washington, it was 1976, and it was puke at first sip – I threw up all over the floor. My happier childhood food memories are endless and specific: tucking in to the aforementioned steak tartare with my father, who would watch me, smiling, and then, inevitably, inform me that I was probably eating horse; mussels, obviously; lobsters on New Year's Eve; *tarte au riz*, a tart filled with nutmegy pudding rice suspended in *crème pâtissière*; and potatoes made of marzipan – balls of marzipan rolled in cocoa dust. These were presented on St Nicholas, 8 December, which is when children got their Christmas presents.

Before the family factory went bankrupt, it held a huge St Nicholas party for the staff and their children; there must have been hundreds of people there. There was a stage and St Nicholas himself, and a horrible blacked-up, rolling-eyed, half-naked creature called Le Père Fouettard, St Nick's evil, un-PC alter ego, whose task it was to whip bad children. Nobody ever got whipped, as far as I can remember, but he was truly terrifying; the smaller children used to cry looking at him. We, the bourgeois offspring of the bosses, were told to behave graciously to the poor children (I can't believe I'm writing this down, but it's all true: 'Be nice to the poor children.') The poor children would stare at us; we'd stare benignly back – really envying their clothes and haircuts, in my case, and the way they ran around, screaming with happiness because they were having such a good time. We didn't run; I sat with one ankle crossed over the other, and my hands in my lap, the ladylike effect slightly spoiled by my hideous, earsy boy's haircut.

STOCKING FILLERS BY POST

Hawkin's Bazaar Browse and buy online at www.hawkin.com. They deliver worldwide and also have retail shops. For inquiries, call: 01986 782536, Mon–Fri, 8.30–5.30; Sat 9–1; longer over Christmas period. They have a huge range of toys, including the Toilet Nanny – an appliance you stick on the loo seat – classic tin toys for adult collectors and good pocket money toys. Nice site.

Letterbox Presents for children, many of which can be personalized – mugs, lunch boxes and so on. Nice range of proper toys – not too much plastic. Browse and buy online at www.letterbox.co.uk; worldwide delivery. For inquiries, call: 0870 600 7878, Mon–Fri, 9–5.30; longer leading up to the Christmas period.

Firebox.com More adult-oriented, but good for boys' toys. Browse and buy online at www.firebox.com; worldwide delivery. For inquiries, call: 0870 241 4289, Mon–Fri, 10–6. They offer lots of headings, such as boys' toys, kitsh, retro and expensive. Site sells Thinking Putty, the Sound Bug, Interactive Jedi Training Light Sabre and the option to buy an acre of moon.

Silly Jokes Like it says – practical jokes, wigs, masks and fancy dress, and who doesn't absolutely *love* whoopee cushions? Browse and buy online at www.sillyjokes.co.uk; delivery to most places – check the website. For inquiries, call: 01327 857839, Mon–Fri, 9–5.

Presents Direct Large range of games and toys for children, plus odd things for the home and garden. Browse and buy online at www.presentsdirect.com; worldwide delivery. For inquiries, call: 020 8246 4355, Mon–Fri, 9–5.

It was a busy period, early December. My uncle René had given some of his land to a priest who ran a home there for what we used to call disadvantaged boys. Fr Robert was the sweetest, kindest man – he still is: he is ancient now, but he buried my father recently, and made very good jokes about my dad's 'love of life', i.e. compulsion to shag women – and he held a St Nicholas party every year for the poor old disadvantageds in my uncle René's living room. Again, we were called upon to grace the occasion. I remember, from quite an early age, thinking that my cousins – I was the only girl in my age group – looked sort of square and dully wholesome compared to the disadvantageds, who were most actively very advantaged indeed when it came to a certain kind of louche glamour.

Anyway, eating your way home. Why should I be so pleased that my eldest son's two absolutely favourite things to eat are mussels and lobster? Why should I have felt a sort of pang in my heart (no, really) when his love of mussels first emerged, aged three? Because I knew where it came from, and it made me glad. My other son is devoted to chocolate: *devoted*. Other children really like chocolate, or sweeties, but he is a passionate obsessive, and can tell the difference between chocolate A and chocolate B at a hundred paces. I recently took the boys to Paris for a weekend and made them try my steak tartare: one refused point blank and accused me of being insane for eating raw cow; the other, helped along by the promise of Asterix books later on, tried a mouthful . . . and then another . . . and another. I was *beaming*.

I feel ambiguous about Brussels – less so now than ten years ago, but still a little bit, because I can't help wondering what would have happened to me if my mother hadn't married my English stepfather and we hadn't moved away. Would I have fulfilled my upper-middle-class destiny, be married to a banker and holiday in the South of France? Would I be one of those women who wear too much jewellery and are too brown and thin? Or would I be a hack and write books on the side – or the other way around –

except in French? God knows, but I don't entirely welcome having to address the question every time I set foot on Belgian soil: it slightly freaks me out.

So I took my boyfriend for a weekend in Brussels with some trepidation: back to the old thing of 'It's OK for me to make jokes, but not for you, because secretly I want you to like it.' We sat in the Grand' Place and I delivered my little lecture about the Dukes of Burgundy and pointed out all the guilds; we wandered about the tiny, medieval streets; we drank beer; we ate like *hogs*. He loved all the food, and, pathetically, by loving all the food I felt he loved me more. On the other hand, he has his own home/food issues, and at a certain point, sitting in a bistro, he put down his fork, stared wildly around him and said, 'We have to stop eating like this. We are turning into *fat bourgeois pigs*.' I think we've seen that he, er, may have had a point. But that's what I mean about eating your way home: not simply that the food I cook when I want to be really nice to my family is the food that was cooked for me as a child; not simply that this is the food I prefer; but that this food is me, and I am it, and there's no getting away from it, bourgeois piggery or no.

Not that we don't all have our secret vices: Findus Crispy Pancakes, in my case (cheese, not mince, there being such things as limits). These were what my lovely paternal grandmother — she of the angora jumper — made for me on weekends, delighted with herself for knowing how to bung frozen orange crumby half-moons into a frying pan and then — wow! — turn them over. I love people's food vices. A friend of mine, an excellent cook who makes her own sushi, had, as a child, a diet consisting mostly of boiled mince, plastic cheese (mmm, plastic cheese. I do *love* it as well, I must say: there's a cheese theme developing) and Fray Bentos pies, the kind you reheated in their half-fabulous, half-grotesque pie-shaped tins. And yes, she can rustle you up a sophisticated little hors-d'oeuvre served on a slice of home-made brioche, and produce extraordinary puddings embellished with spun sugar and orange-flower water, but she still really loves those Fray Bentos pies. Brillat-Savarin's dictum – 'Tell me what you eat and I will tell you who you are' – holds true: we may be able to train ourselves to eat raw sea urchin without gagging (yummy, actually, eventually), but we all have our Fray Bentos moments.

We've all seen those middle-class women at Sainsbury's, hiding the Angel Delight or tinned fruit – the Food of Shame – under the super-deluxe, made-by-genuine-peasants focaccia. Actually, we've all *been* those women. And not just women: a distinguished former food critic I know used to go into spasms of ecstasy at the very idea of the sulphurous, farty Brussels sprouts on offer every day at the British Medical Association canteen.

PANTS OF STEEL

Let's not beat around the bush: if you eat like a pig, you look like a pig, or at least some portions of you do, such as the rump and the belly (belly is a strong contender for my least favourite word,* but I'm trying to go with the pig analogy). At this point, you can go on a diet, of course, but I'm guessing that more instant measures might be called for. It's all very well going on diets, but some mornings you just wake up fat and have a party to go to that night. What do you need? Pants of Steel. When do you need them? NOW. But there are a few things you need to know. The thing about Pants of Steel is that, bizarrely, not all of them work. They all function along the same principle: compress the flesh, reduce the waist/thigh/stomach line. But what I have discovered, in my long years of association with these most unfrivolous of underthings, is that, while all species of steel pant do indeed compress and reduce, it is a rare pant that doesn't redistribute the flesh to another, wholly unwelcome, area — which is how you end up with weird wodges of podge on, say, your lower back, or halfway down your thighs (with minimizer bras, the surfeit normally reappears in pert, compact little rolls just by your armpits — f.o.x.y.). Now, I can't explain why this podge redistribution should be a side-effect of some pants but not of others — you'd think it was a given with all pants, a fundamental pant truth. But no. Pay attention now: the pants you want are by Nancy Gantz and they're called BodySlimmers. The one you're after is the Hi-Waist BellyBuster (yes, I know, not lovely), a.k.a. style 6301, which at the time of writing costs £19 and is widely

---

 * Also moist, gusset — moist gusset, aaaargh — nibble, gusto, titbit, cheesy, tasty, superb. The sentence 'This superb cheese is really tasty' makes me want to keel over.

available from www.figleaves.com, John Lewis and its siblings, Harrods, Selfridges, Debenhams and House of Fraser stores. Quite miraculously, these can — and do — take a couple of inches off your waist and stop you looking like you're four months pregnant, without the excess flesh making an unwelcome reappearance elsewhere. *I don't know whether it's a question of Lycra content or more of a design thing, but they really, really work where all other PoSs have failed. If you have that English hip and thigh thing, whereby you look like you're wearing jodhpurs even when you're naked, they do a longer-line steel pant that will have you weeping with gratitude. There's a whole range, to cover every need, including some very hefty constructions that go from the bosom down. Needless to say, these garments are not remotely comfy to wear — though they don't actually cut off your circulation in the way that lesser Pants of Steel do — and are more of a special-occasion accessory than a daily staple. But who cares, really, when they mean you can cram your flooby post-partum waist and abdomen into a size 12 and feel like a total minx, if only for one night? Also, they don't look as bad as they sound: like minimalist plain black boxers. I mean, you wouldn't proudly strut about in them in front of your new boyfriend, huskily murmuring, 'Lick my panties', but you wouldn't actually die of shame if he found them on the bathroom floor either. Blush beetroot and have to leave at once, maybe. Die, no.*

THE FOOD OF SHAME, DELIVERED
TO YOU IN PLAIN BROWN WRAPPERS

Supermarkets are getting increasingly snooty about their stock, and
you can't guarantee they'll still stock all your vices. Iceland does.
You can order online at www.iceland.co.uk, or get a catalogue. Hello,
disgusting biscuits filled with marshmallow. Hello, Findus-fest.
Frozen cheesecake, I love you. Oooh, tinned faggots . . . Bring it on.

For many of us, the Food of Shame is chocolate, or variants
thereof. I don't care for it much — my worst food vice is cheese,
especially stinky cheese, which I am able to consume in inhuman
quantities — even though chocolate is synonymous with Belgium,
and even though it was omnipresent in my childhood: you didn't
go anywhere without stopping off at Godiva first. When my
mother moved to London, and I went to visit my dear papa in
the school holidays, I always had to bring back boxes of Godiva
chocolates, especially the dark ones filled with pineapple, cream
and liqueur. I've tried to love chocolate in a serious way, because
I feel it is my duty as a Belgian passport holder, but I can only
feel lackadaisical about it (there is one lone and magnificent
exception: see page 64). Sure, I'll eat it — my chocolate of choice
is the very English, very grannyish rose or violet cream — but I'll
only have one, not half the box, and I like cheap chocolate better
than the posh stuff. Still, I do know the difference between cheap
and expensive, mass-produced and handmade — I've been round
the factories and done the tastings, as everyone who spends time
in Brussels does at some point — and I know what you want in a
really good chocolate.

THE BEST BELGIAN CHOCOLATES, AND THE ONES TO AVOID

Neuhaus is the best Belgian *chocolatier* and the oldest (www.neuhauschocolate.com, US only; UK from http://www.ishop.co.uk/ishop/554/shopscr32.html, among others, but not the whole range). Neuhaus, not Godiva, although Godiva comes second. Don't even think of shopping at the ghastly, touristy Leonidas — and for God's sake, avoid those brown-and-white shells you can pick up everywhere. They're not the real thing. For cooking (supposedly — it's still my favourite milk chocolate in the world), stock up on Côte d'Or chocolate from supermarkets (lovely packaging).

ENGLISH CHOCOLATE

Rococo 321 Kings Road, London SW3 5EP; tel: 020 7352 5857.
Open: Mon–Sat, 10–6.30; Sun, 12–5. Fabulous, fabulous chocolate.
Geranium-scented paper-thin chocolate wafers; extraordinary,
baroque-tasting cardamom truffles; organic artisan bars in flavours
such as Earl Grey, thyme, cinnamon. Sugar-free sweeties to lob at
your children. Dairy-free and vegan stuff available also. Browse and
buy online at www.rococochocolates.com – though not the whole
range, as some of it, including the above wafers, is too delicate to
post. There's a mail-order catalogue too; they'll ship pretty much
everywhere. And they can make individual one-off art pieces.

Prestat 14 Princes Arcade, Piccadilly, London SW1Y 6DS;
tel: 020 7629 4838. Open: Mon–Fri, 9.30–6; Sat, 10–5. Yum-yum.
Divine rose and violet creams, truffles (including banoffee) and
a lovely thing called the Heart Box – a beautiful object in itself –
which you fill with your selection (online at www.prestat.co.uk)
and have sent to your beloved for roughly £20. Exquisite packaging.
Ships worldwide. Queen's chocolate supplier (ooo). Very, very
magnificent Easter eggs.

THE WHITE MANON
The Only Chocolate That Can Make You Sob with Joy

Oh, my goodness. The white Manon is, in my opinion, the most extraordinary chocolate in the world. Each one (handmade) is an incredibly decadent-looking off-white blob of loveliness. Bite through the thin, sugary shell and your teeth sink into another thin layer of white chocolate of such an extraordinary texture — fluffy and solid at the same time — that all I can say, pseudily, is that it feels completely eighteenth century, and leave it at that. Eventually, you reach the cream — sweet, white, contrasting with the crispy-yet-fondant outside . . . At which point you swoon. Right at the bottom of the Manon is a walnut half. I am rendered inarticulate with love over these things: I really mean it about sobbing with joy. There is something literally transporting about them. I know how odd and crazily grandiloquent that sounds, but it is true — they are other-worldly. Only Neuhaus make them properly. If you are going to Brussels, you must, must, must bring some back.

I'm not entirely done with food: it pops up in unexpected
places. If you're after something specific that isn't covered in
this chapter, check the Index. Kitchen equipment – pans and
so on – are in the home chapter.

Looking Better

First off, I am not a beauty expert, though I am a beauty junkie. I did have a brief stint writing about beauty products, which I enjoyed tremendously, but I want to make it clear that I am not a beauty editor, have never worked in the beauty industry, don't specialize in writing about lip gloss — you get the picture. If you're after a genuine beauty bible, compiled and written by people who really know their stuff, get the accurately named *21st Century Beauty Bible*, by Sarah Stacey and Josephine Fairley.* It is *bliss*, very useful, heaven to read in the bath, and packed to the gills with information. Their website is good too: www.thebeautybible.com.

Elsewhere, do please bear in mind that editorial coverage of beauty products in your favourite glossy magazine is inextricably and fundamentally linked to advertising, that no glossies can survive without advertising, *ergo* that if X's new cosmetics line is an utter disaster, you're unlikely to read a trenchant critique in *Lovely Me* magazine.† When I worked on a glossy, in the early 1990s, we'd shoot the cover girl and then simply invent whatever products the make-up artist was supposed to have used on her to match the brand name of the expensive ad on the back cover. So if Dior had spent thousands and thousands advertising on the back, we'd say the make-up used on Miss Supermodel was by Dior. We made it up. Everyone does a blue eyeshadow: the stuff used in the picture may have been by Maybelline, but we'd say it was Bleu Fabuleux, or whatever, by C. Dior. I used to wonder about the poor girl who'd saved up to buy the lipstick Christy Turlington was supposed to be wearing, and who'd ask herself why it looked so different on her.

---

* Kyle Cathie, £25, but out in paperback by the time this comes out, I expect.
† *Lovely Me* is actually the name of Barbara Seaman's biography of the late Jacqueline Susann — as in *Valley of the Dolls* — and it is well worth seeking out second-hand if your tastes run to camp.

None of which is to say there aren't excellent beauty writers around, because there are (Newby Hands of *Harpers & Queen* is worth the cover price alone), but they are the exception rather than the rule. It remains a fact that your average beauty article is quite likely to be a clumsy rehash of a press release from some multinational beauty corporation, passing on to you, the reader, only what said multinational wants you to know — i.e. that its product is revolutionary. Yeah, yeah. The nuisance with this is that you get boy who cried wolf syndrome: no doubt some products really are exceptional, but they become lost in the torrent of hysterical praise heaped upon absolutely everything else.

In beauty, like elsewhere, what you really want to know is what works. You are unlikely to find this out from any source that needs megabucks cosmetics advertising revenue to survive. You won't necessarily find it out from me either — my recommendations are, obviously, entirely subjective: they are what works for me. But I'm giving it my best shot — we have a lifetime's findings coming up — so read on; and do also visit the utterly fantastic **www.makeupalley.com** message boards — discussions on everything from really obscure scent to the best red nail polish, from informed, intelligent, literate punters. It gets very addictive. For serious, useful, take-no-prisoners reviews of products, subscribe to Heather Kleinman's Cosmetic Connection at **www.cosmeticconnections.com**. You'll get a weekly e-mail reviewing a specific line and access to a searchable database of reviews. Kleinman really knows her onions.

There is an especial joy in shopping for make-up and other beauty products: namely, you're never too fat, too short, too thin (oh, boo hoo) — and, given that cheap make-up is very often the business, you are seldom too broke.

- Ruby and Millie's range of make-up, widely available from a number of places, including Boots. Utterly brilliant, even the foundations. Everything works, is beautifully packaged and designed, and is, in terms of colours and textures, as cutting-edge, if not more so, than designer ranges which cost three times as much.

- Vaseline, our old pal. Still gives the glossiest, least sticky lips (mix it with some lipstick if you want a bit of discreet oomph), fixes horrible dry patches on elbows, smoothes frizzy hair in emergencies, and looks fab slicked on eyelids for night-time (not in nightclubs – it melts if too hot). The little 99p tin is particularly dinky and lovable, and belongs in everyone's handbag. Or crank it up a notch moneywise with Smith's Rosebud Salve, which does all of the above but is rose-scented and comes in the prettiest tin – from any US chemist (cheap cheap) or www.missgroovy.co.uk.

- Bourjois eyeshadows. I've loved these since I was about thirteen. Terrific colours and they smell delicious. Much cheaper in France. The blushers aren't bad either.

- Max Factor 2000 Calorie mascara. See page 95.

- Maybelline eye pencils – soft, smudgy, don't slide off, cheaporama.

- Fat glitter pencils by Urban Decay – they do one in soft gold that's brilliant on eyelids and looks really slick and 'finished', even if you're clumsy – and others.

- If you're a fan of kohl, go to an Asian shop and buy a pack of kohl powder and a silver vial (with – scary-looking but actually foolproof – stalk-like applicator) to keep it in. No other product does sooty and sultry as well or effortlessly as this, *and* it's good for your eyes, unlike the stuff in pencil form. Lasts years.

If you're in the US, look out for the following mass-market lines:

- Apartment 5 Cosmetics, from omnipresent drug-store chain Duane Reade, especially the blushers and mascaras.

- Black Opal (for 'women of colour'): terrific, with particularly fine powders and, unusually, foundations.

- Jane, which is like cheap MAC, i.e. total heaven.

- Prestige: fab lip glosses and eyeshadows.

You can be too young, though. I was never allowed to wear make-up and my schoolfriends were: at primary school in London, I remember gazing with agonized longing at my friend Catriona's make-up bag – a grubby fluffy pencil case – which represented to me the absolute acme of sophistication. She lived, with her mother and older sister, just down the road from school (we were both at the Lycée in London, but Catriona was English), and her mother – fabulous, with a jet-black beehive, sooty eyes and a dancer's body – would smile indulgently as we played with her make-up. Catriona wore mascara on her huge hyacinth-blue eyes, *and* lipstick, *and* blusher. I was completely bare-faced, and completely envious. I *knew* everything there was to know about make-up, the cosmetics counters exercising as strong a pull as the stationer's, and could tell a Dior lipstick from a Chanel at a hundred paces.

This was in no small part because I had by this time acquired a stepmother, Anne, whose life was devoted to cosmetic enhancement. She took tanning pills, and so had orange palms; she wore frosted eyeshadow of the kind considered unspeakably vulgar by my mother, and three coats of mascara; she had, shall we say, unsubtly streaked hair; she went to the gym before anyone else I knew; she sunbathed topless (I remember being ten and surreptitiously studying her nipples on the beach); she had

'treatments' every day; she was *permanently* on a diet of small yoghurts. Her regime would have killed another kind of woman. I liked her — she was like a creature, and very kind to me. Anne suffered from constipation, and every summer at the seaside, I'd get the breakfast *petits pains* (which she didn't eat — she had an early and morbid fear of carbohydrates) and, on my return, solicitously inquire about her morning evacuations:

— *Ça a été, Anne?*

— *Non. Pas de succès.*

She'd look downcast, so would I, and a gloomy atmosphere would descend upon the breakfast table. (Incidentally, I don't recommend discussing your morning poos over the Frosties. It's really, really unsexy. I want my boyfriend to believe that I'm such a goddess of fox that I don't even *have* bowel movements. This may sound old-fashioned, but I don't care. I have enough male friends to know that companionable poo-chats do little for the male libido. Poo-chats lead to pal-sex — as in, if you were a bloke he'd thwack you appreciatively on the back, but since you're not, he'll go for a half-hearted, matey shag instead.)

Later — much, much later, when Anne had left my father because he ran out of money and had shacked up with a very rich, very fat man (Anne, I mean, not my dad) — the man was the fattest I'd ever met in a double-bed context: it was awful to think of anyone you knew actually doing it with him — I realized that the gold razor blade she wore around her neck wasn't exclusively decorative. I also realized — I was seventeen, and the shock of it practically made me pass out — that my father and she had liked, Frenchly, group sex — swapping, swinging, going to strange sex parties in strange houses. I realized because, over a pre-dinner drink, she cheerfully showed me photographs of these parties — I was, after all, 'an adult now' — flicking the thick pages of the leather-bound album with a manicured finger. She wasn't remotely trying to freak me out, I don't think — she, my father and her new partner, Mr Porky, were all giggling indulgently at the photos, as though to say, 'Goodness, double penetration, weren't we silly.' Then the album went away and we carried on making small talk. I sometimes think I must have imagined this event, but I kept a diary at the time and, having just consulted it, know for a fact that I didn't. Now, I think that people who want to have group sex should go right ahead, and a part of me can absolutely see the appeal; but seeing your father's penis peering out of a photograph is perhaps best avoided if you are a sensitive adolescent. It was absolutely massive, which really didn't help (or perhaps it did: if I have to think about my father's penis, I'd rather it was sizeable than humiliatingly minute, I *suppose*). My father was extremely devoted to sex, as evidenced not only by his marriages, hundreds of girlfriends and so on, but also by his massive collection of pornography. There were thousands of back issues all over his apartment, in neat, orderly piles. He used to read *Playboy* and *Lui* quite casually, as the family gathered for a pre-prandial *aperitif*, which makes me laugh to myself as I type. I love the idea of him making distinctions between what was and what wasn't acceptable reading matter in front of one's great-aunt in one of Europe's most staunchly Catholic countries: *Playboy*, yes, *Anal Sluts*, no.

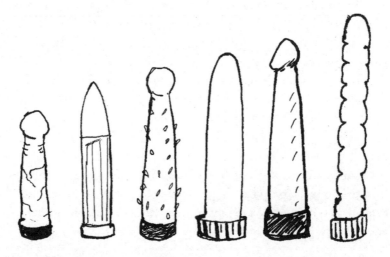

SEX AIDS

Oooh, dirt. The best-stocked and most comfortable sex shop I know is Sh!, 39 Coronet Street, London N1 6HD; tel: 020 7613 5458. Open: Mon–Sat, 10–8; Sun, 10–5. Browse at www.sh-womenstore.com. They ship everywhere. It is comfortable because it is women-run and women-only, i.e. you don't get any horrible mouth-breathers standing next to you, panting. Shopping in a women-only environment is very jolly, in this case – there's often a feeling of barely suppressed hysteria (or maybe it's just me), and other people's recommendations are hugely entertaining as well as informative. Staff are extremely friendly – just as well, as this is hardly the kind of place you'd want frosty service – and also helpful, chatty and knowledgeable. The shop is clean and bright pink, which is always a plus, and they don't sell junk. I'm not going to make recommendations – too much information, I feel – but I do really recommend the shop itself. And they don't mind if you start laughing like a loon – if you're in the next changing room to a cheery lezzer trying on a gigantic strap-on, say.

If you're abroad, Sonia Rykiel's daughter Nathalie runs a very deluxe and chic sex shop, called Woman, at 4 rue de Grenelle in Paris, though I must say I don't really like the sudden proliferation of chic sex shops that sell £300 designer vibrators and display them on marble plinths. You want a bit of cheek, I think, not a lot of po-face, in a sex shop. Still, this one is worth a visit, because it is *so* French.

If you're too shy to turn up in person (bless), have a look at the women-run www.goodvibes.com, the online sibling to the well-known San Francisco store Good Vibrations. The site is intelligent, informative (take a look at the Vibrator Museum section) and makes you feel rather *Our Bodies, Our Selves*-ish and in charge of your own sexual destiny – it's not un-wimminish. Go on, have a peek – but do bear in mind that ordering stuff from the US sometimes involves paying a fee to Customs & Excise. And sometimes it doesn't. It's completely random, so you just have to keep your fingers crossed until the law changes.

Anyway, the point is that I wasn't allowed to wear make-up for ages. Eventually, my mother made one small (to her — it was vast to me) concession: I could wear kohl, because it was Indian and so was I. What she didn't quite register, I don't think, was that kohl was, in the mid-1970s, absolutely where it was at eye-wise, and so I whooped with joy, crammed as much of it as I could into my eyes and went off, skipping. The application of kohl sparked a lifelong devotion to every kind of make-up.

After I'd had my first child, I felt like a beached whale for months — a very happy beached whale, but a beached whale none the less. My post-Caesarean stomach, which had been pretty convex even pre-pregnancy, left quite a lot to be desired. Feeling fat, frumpy and mumsy, I got back into make-up big time (this wasn't a first: I spent my teens in sooty false eyelashes and my university career sporting a faux beauty spot just below my left eye. I had the feeling I was rather divinely eighteenth century. Oh *dear* — youth). But that's what I so love about make-up: you may feel like you're never going to have a normal body again, you may wince when you sit down, you may be knackered all the time — but then you go out to dinner wearing glittery green eyeshadow and you feel much better. Also, unlike the more dramatic forms of transformation, if it looks crap you can just wash it off.

PREGNANT? LOOK NICE: BUY YOUR CLOTHES HERE

A Pea in the Pod Online clothes for pregnant women. Browse and buy online at www.apeainthepod.com. Selections include designer wear, such as Diane Von Furstenberg (hooray! her dresses are perfect for your condition, believe me), office wear that isn't direly naff, and lounge wear. Located in Macys, New York. They will ship worldwide, but Canada and international are subject to a brokerage fee; e-mail them via the website for details. There's a weird thing going on with stuff shipped from America to do with UK Customs, which can randomly choose to impose extra tax but very often don't.

Formes 33 Brook Street, London W1K 4HG; tel: 020 7493 2783. Open: Mon–Wed, 10–6; Thurs, 10–7; Fri, Sat, 10–6.30. Bit solemn for me – very French – but people swear by it. Excellent trousers with ingenious expanding waistband system: not the usual enormous one-size-fits-all 'front gusset' arrangement, but buttons and straps that grow with you. Browse and buy online at www.formes.com. They deliver practically worldwide; for inquiries and help, call: 020 8689 1133, Mon–Fri, 9–6.

Jojo Maman Bébé 3 Ashbourne Parade, 1259 Finchley Road, London NW11 0AD; tel: 020 8731 8961. Open: Mon–Sat, 9.30–5.30; Sun, 10–4. Lovely and affordable maternity wear, clothes and toys for small children and babies. Browse and buy online at www.jojomamanbebe.co.uk. Worldwide delivery; for inquiries, call: 0870 160 8820, Mon–Fri, 9–5.

Hennes & Mauritz Largest store: 103–111 High Street Kensington, London W8 5SF; tel: 020 7368 3920. Open: Mon–Sat, 10–7 (Thurs, 8); Sun, 12–6. Not the first place you think of when pregnant, but they have a great and remarkably cheap range called Mama. Browse it online at www.hm.com (the site has a search facility to help you find your nearest stockist) or call: 020 7323 2211, Mon–Fri, 9–5.

Harry Duley Very nicely designed sexy, stretchy, comfy maternity wear, non-maternity wear and brightly coloured children's wear. You can browse online at www.harryduley.co.uk. For inquiries, catalogues and to order, call: 020 7485 5552, Mon–Fri, 10–6, or

e-mail: info@harryduley.co.uk. Each item is made to order, which takes 14 days, and is shown in black on the website but comes in different colourways (swatches in the catalogue), and because it's all made of stretch (92% cotton, 8% Lycra), you don't need to dump it once you've popped the sprog out. Brilliant for travelling too.

Pleats Please by Issey Miyake Tightly pleated trousers, tunics and shift dresses that look good whether you're big or small, pregnant or not, in wonderful colours. See www.pleatsplease.com for all details of stockists and inquiries. A favourite with the larger person – see page 170 for more on this – but NB the frocks can look quite sack-like unless you're wearing a proper bra (which you'll find on page 168).

Ghost The bias cutting and stretchiness of the fabric means that these easy, stylish, boho clothes look as good on pregnant elephants as they do on size 6 waifs. No specific pregnancy range, but all of the basics would look terrific. I wear a Ghost uniform in the summer: you can pack two weeks' worth of clothes in a little holdall. See www.ghost.co.uk for current collections and the opportunity to buy selected items; also for stockists and to print out a mail-order form (there is no mail-order catalogue).

The very cornerstone of looking good is, indisputably, good skin, which is why there are hundreds of different foundations, concealers and bases on the market. Good skin is the nirvana of make-up. Ironically enough, what all we make-up junkies want is to have the kind of dermis that makes make-up an optional extra. What most of us have to make do with is the kind of skin that's pretty so-so *au naturel* but not so bad that it can't be perfectly concealed — that is, given the appearance of perfection — with foundation.

First things first. I'd say, don't go there unless you absolutely have to, i.e. unless you've tried every skin-improving cleanser and potion and failed (you don't *really* have to try every single one: I've made you a list — see page 80). Work on the skin first, not on the camouflage. Like any tricks involving gel-filled breast pads or tinted contact lenses, covering up your real skin with faux skin out of a tube means you're only going to disappoint ultimately (this is a euphemism for 'at bedtime'). Nobody wants to be the sort of woman who turns from peach to pasty, blotchy wreck when she washes her face — which is why many of us have slept in foundation every now and then over the years to impress some Mr Lover-Lover or other, even though we knew this was a dermatologically disastrous course of action. Please don't do this: the foundation smears into the pillow, which makes you look dirty and slapperish (there are better ways, and better accessories than smeary skin: see Sex Aids box, page 73); the bits that don't end up in the bedding end up blocking your pores; and, most crucially, slept-in foundation makes doing the Walk of Shame — the getting home the following morning — far more sordid than it need be.

Good skin starts with good cleansing. I really think I've tried them all, the cleansers, over the years, waiting for The One. I finally found it aged thirty-seven, rather in the manner of a Barbara Pym heroine finally finding love with a curate. It is called Cleanse and Polish Hot Cloth Cleanser, it is made by the former beauty journalist Liz Earle, it is quasi-organic, and it has totally changed my skin — the dry bits aren't dry any more, the oily bits appear normal, my skin feels squeaky-clean but not tight or stripped, and my face just looks more even, somehow. It's not expensive, either (see box), and because Liz Earle works by mail or online ordering, provided you have a phone you can get it by the day after tomorrow even if you live in the Outer Hebrides. You use it with a muslin cloth, which means you don't need to exfoliate separately. (The muslin cloth is where it's at, really, no matter what cleanser you use — buy them cheap in the baby department of any big store, and please wash them after two uses, not, as a friend of mine does, weekly — urgh.)

You'll notice my box is heavy on the 'natural' products and low on the high-tech. That's because I don't personally believe in putting dodgy — or even undodgy — chemicals on my (absorbent, porous — der!) skin. I have the kind of skin that flares up dramatically at the smallest provocation. I can't use most normal bubble baths, and if I'm stressed, for instance, I get weird rashes. I'm sure all those creams and potions with magical-sounding properties and names that are supposed to be terribly convincing and scientific work for some people — it's just they don't work for me, and besides I find them obscurely creepy.

BEST CLEANSERS

This is, of course, completely subjective – even more subjective than the rest of the book. You need to know about my skin: I have weird skin – my nose and chin are oily, and everything else is both dry and sensitive. I come up in rashes at the slightest provocation. I like washing cleansers off; I don't feel clean if I use only cotton wool. And I like stuff that's capable of shifting a faceload of make-up – even if I don't wear that much every day, I want to feel that my cleanser is big and strong and TOUGH, as well as natural and coy and girly.

- **Liz Earle Cleanse and Polish** Does everything, doesn't cost the earth, is lovely to use, works. I love this. Only from www.lizearle.net or by phone on 01983 813 913. Worldwide delivery. For customer services, follow-ups, questions and advice, call: 01983 813 999. Both lines Mon–Fri, 8.30–8; Sat, 9–4.

- **Eve Lom Cleanser** The original revolutionary odd-to-use waxy pomade, removed with a muslin cloth. Comes with instructions for facial massage. Very good: you really do feel squeaky-clean after this, but I find it's a bit full-on for my skin in winter. On the other hand, I know people with terrible skin whose sad dermis has been transformed into a thing of beauty solely by using this product. Buy online at www.evelom.com; worldwide delivery.

- **Ultrabland by Lush** Yes, the hippieish shops that make you feel fourteen. Not a bad product at all, this – their version of Eve Lom – though I'd say better suited to drier skins. Gets absolutely everything off, including camouflage paint. As long as you tone very thoroughly afterwards – it's madly waxy – you should get pretty great results. Also, very, very cheap, and lasts ages – you use a pea-sized amount. Browse and buy online at www.lush.co.uk; for inquiries, call: 01202 668 545, Mon–Fri, 9–7; Sat, 10–4. For Lush shops and shipping worldwide, check details on website.

- **Amanda Lacey Cleansing Pomade** Not a million miles from Eve Lom's – I actually prefer it, and it's less faffy to use. Get it from Amanda Lacey Mail Order on 020 7370 4410; worldwide delivery.

- **Dr Hauschka's Cleansing Cream** A sort of grainy cleansing ointment, this is excellent if you can stand its weird, beery smell. Their Cleansing Milk is gentle, delicious and works beautifully.

Browse and buy online at www.drhauschka.co.uk (also use the site to look up their accredited facialists). For inquiries, mail order and catalogues, call: 01386 792622, Mon–Fri, 9–5.30. They're good at doling out specific advice and are very friendly.

I should make special mention here of a cleanser called **Cetaphil**. This is what you should use if your skin is a disaster, or hypersensitive – if you have eczema,* say, or have (sun)burnt yourself, or if you suddenly start developing allergies. It's the cleanser dermatologists recommend for women who've just had plastic surgery: incredibly gentle, but gets everything off. The maddening thing about Cetaphil is that it is a timorous beastie and doesn't advertise itself, so you usually have to order it from your chemist – if you tell them it's made by a company called Galderma, they can look it up (and can normally get it in for you within a couple of days). It's very cheap and comes in an unlovely plastic bottle, but it really does the business. NB: If you're going to the States, Cetaphil is available in every drug store, even cheaper and marginally more attractively packaged (with pump dispenser). I find it too emollient to use every day, because I have combination skin, but if you have dry sensitive skin that hates ordinary cleansers, this is going to be your new best friend.

So, use a decent cleanser, moisturize – but not madly: I've never, for instance, met anyone who needed to moisturize their nose or chin, though I've met lots of people who wonder why they have nose and chin blackheads and otherwise perfect skin – and try to visit a facialist every now and then if you possibly can. It's expensive and self-indulgent, but it really does make a dramatic difference.

* In which case, see also page 13.

BEST TONERS

The best toner I have ever come across is very cold water. I really mean this. Splash it on to your face at least twenty times in the morning and twenty at night, and then tell me I'm wrong. If you must have something from a bottle, Liz Earle's toner and Dr Hauschka's are both nice. But not as good as cold water.

Apologies if the box that follows is London-centric (it's more or less the only one, I hope), but London is where I live, and besides all of the facialists listed below are more than worth a Day Return. And again, I implore you, if they seem expensive – which they are – get friends and relatives to club together to book you a treatment. People are far too undemanding about birthdays: a really top facial costs the same as two not especially lovely bottles of scent and a bunch of garage flowers. Or a dinner for two. Which you get is up to you – I'd rather have the peachy skin.

BEST FACIALISTS

- **Vashailly Patel**, see page 20.
- **Amanda Lacey**, see page 80.
- **Renate at Renate**, 4 Cheval Place, London SW7 1ES; tel: 020 7589 1133; e-mail: renatestudio@talk21.com. She'll try and fit in with you, so no opening hours given. Absolutely the best Dr Hauschka facials* – Renate herself is an amazing advertisement. No extraction (see page 83, she's the exception to my rule), but my goodness you leave looking *fabulous*. Renate also does facials for people with acne – you need to have one every fortnight – and performs miracles where all else has failed. She also practises homeopathy to help acne sufferers.

* Though see also the list of accredited facialists at www.drhauschka.co.uk.

There are all sorts of different facials available. My theory is that,
lovely as it is to have your face pummelled and massaged with rose oil,
it doesn't actually do a huge amount of good when it comes to seeing
the difference a few days later. I like — like is the wrong word: I am
impressed by (grossly) — extraction facials, where pores are unblocked,
rubbish removed with tools, skin squeezed, and you come out with
what looks like new skin. To me, having a facial means having a
treatment that I couldn't carry out at home myself. Incidentally,
assuming you have normal-ish skin, a good facialist should leave you
radiant and ready to go straight out, not spotty or red or covered in
oily unguents. And for goodness' sake, have a look at your facialist's
skin before lying down, and use your common sense. I once went for
a facial in Dickins and Jones which was administered by a woman with
throbbing facial pustules (also she breathed through her mouth, like
a rapist). Very sad for her, but really horrid for me. If the products
they're using on you aren't working on them, why bother?

So you've got your skin sorted out, we hope (give it at least a month,
which is how long it takes for skin cells to renew themselves). It's time to
gild the lily. It goes without saying that the rather bossy directions that
follow on page 88 are what work for me — they may not work if you're
my physical opposite, e.g. a pocket-sized platinum blonde. Though
I don't see why not.

SCENT

I don't want to smell like everybody else. I want to smell like me, and me only, which means I want a scent that's only mine — or as good as. I want The One. This is partly galloping egomania and partly to do with the unhappy fact that most scents nowadays are not only crudely composed but actually smell horribly artificial — plasticky, even. I didn't used to feel nauseous when standing in the lift at M&S ten years ago, but I do now, because everyone seems to have drenched themselves in ghastly cheap perfume (even when it's expensive) that smells, incredibly potently, of air freshener. Actually, I'll just come out and say it: I think most scent today smells common. The idea of complexity or evocativeness seems to have disappeared from the perfume-maker's art, and to have been replaced with naff — and usually synthetic — scents that might be more effectively used in the manufacturing of lip gloss for ten-year-old girls: vanilla, chocolate, fruit, in industrial quantities. Those great fragrances of the past — some, like Guerlain's L'Heure Bleue or Après l'Ondée, almost unbearably evocative — have been pushed aside in favour of tacky gimmicks that smell like poo-masker. And I can't understand it. Do women spray on Generic Perfume A and truly feel enveloped by loveliness, comforted, reinforced? A really good scent is an amazing thing, with almost narcotic qualities: it makes you feel sexy, complicated, alluring, confident, ready to take the world on. Unless you were particularly simple-minded, I just can't see how smelling of synthetic chocolate would have the same effect. And yet today's most commercially successful scents either fall into this category or smell 'fresh' and 'clean', which usually means abrasively citric. Given that I wash regularly, I don't want to smell extra clean, personally — I like scents that are a little bit dirty and complicated. You wouldn't wear giant, waist-high white cotton knickers when out on a hot date, would you? So why smell of their olfactory equivalent?

But all is not lost. Great fragrances are still being made and sold, and not all are impossibly tricky to get hold of. The old, great Guerlain scents—Jicky, Shalimar, L'Heure Bleue, Après l'Ondée, Mitsouko, Nahema, Vol de Nuit*— are still widely available in department stores and duty-free lounges. Chanel's warm, sexy, smoky, leathery Cuir de Russie is available from its boutiques (I don't like it quite as much as Caron's Tabac Blond, but it's easier to come by—and it beats No. 5 hands down). Shiseido do some amazing scents that you can find in department stores, including Feminité du Bois. Harrods, my least favourite shop, does have an amazing perfumery department that stocks unique scents not available elsewhere, including the aforementioned Tabac Blond (and Narcisse Noir, if you want to smell like a 1930s femme fatale—and who, frankly, wouldn't?). And the Internet is an excellent tool for tracking down scents that are hard to come by, provided you know what you want—see below, and do check out the discussion boards on www.makeupalley.com, which are essential if you are the kind of person whose mission to track down The One is slightly obsessive.

Note of warning: Women go mad for the scent of tuberose, which really is narcotic—I used to drown myself in Fracas before having children, when some hormonal change occurred and now the merest whiff of it makes me gag. Anyway, in my subsequent experience, it has sadly come to my attention that nine out of ten men loathe tuberose, and have cruel things to say about women who wear it. Do please remember that scent shouldn't be headache-inducing: the idea is that people catch a whiff of your divine, alluring fragrance close up and swoon with pleasure, not that they're hit over the head with it whenever they come within 100 yards of you and have to run away, retching.

My personal scent favourites, in no particular order: Après l'Ondée by Guerlain; Jasmin Vert by Miller Harris; Bal à Versailles by Jean Desprez; Vol de Nuit by Guerlain; Tabac Blond by Caron; Quel Amour by Annick Goutal; Jasmin and Or des Indes by Maître Parfumeur et Gantier; Feminité du Bois by Shiseido.

 * Also Mouchoir de Monsieur, the best men's scent ever. Only available from horrible Harrods, alas, and you have to save up for it.

WHERE TO GET IT FROM: SOME IDEAS

L'Artisan Parfumeur 17 Cale Street, Chelsea, London SW3 3QR; tel: 020 7352 4196. Open: Mon–Fri, 10–6; Sat, 10–5.30. Yummy, pretty, and shouldn't frighten the horses. Browse and buy online at UK site at www.mkn.co.uk/perfume. Can deliver worldwide. They provide a scent sample service. Concessions in London at Liberty's, Harvey Nichols, Fenwick, House of Fraser and Harrods.

Editions de Parfums Frédéric Malle 37 rue de Grenelle, 75007 Paris; tel: +33 1 42 22 77 22. Open: Mon–Fri, 11–7 (Paris time). Amazing. M. Malle gave several world-class 'noses' carte blanche to produce their perfect fragrance, regardless of expense, marketing and all the things that usually place terrible restrictions on creating a fantastic scent. Perfumes and body lotions. Browse and buy online on this very comprehensive website at www.editionsdeparfums.com; there's a marvellous bit where you answer a very French questionnaire and they e-mail you back suggestions. They do a scent called Lipstick Rose which makes me gag slightly – it's very sweet, in both senses – but is the most amazing man-magnet. Worldwide delivery.

Floris 89 Jermyn Street, London SW1Y 6JH; tel: 020 7930 2885. Open: Mon–Fri, 9.30–6; Sat, 10–6. A beautiful shop, with Spanish mahogany showcases acquired in the Great Exhibition of 1851. Queen Victoria used to use Floris fragrance on a lace handkerchief. Floris is the oldest perfumer in London. Old-fashioned, divine fragrances for men and women. Also sells accessories and home fragrances. Browse and buy online at www.florislondon.co.uk; worldwide delivery. For inquiries, call: 0845 702 3239, Mon–Fri, 9.30–5.30. Concessions in London at Fortnum and Mason, Harrods, House of Fraser, John Lewis, Liberty and Peter Jones.

Les Senteurs 71 Elizabeth Street, London SW1W 9PJ; tel: 020 7730 2322. Open: Mon–Sat, 10–6. Specialist perfumery. For women, men and home. My favourite fragrance shop, with astonishingly good and well-chosen stock. The shop is beautiful and the staff very knowledgeable and friendly; you can spend hours in here. Mail order by catalogue (which is a pleasure to read) or over the phone; they will post worldwide. They also offer a sample service – tell them what you like the sound of from the catalogue and they'll decant some for you and send it.

See also fragrances by Miller Harris (from the eponymous W11 shop; tel: 020 7221 1545), Annick Goutal (via Liberty) and Creed (Liberty and others). And don't forget Penhaligon's Bluebell – though no one who's read *I Capture the Castle* (see page 108) ever could.

If you're in Florence, please go to the Officina Profumo-Farmaceutica di Santa Maria Novella, Via della Scala 16/r, tel: +39 55 216276, which is housed in a frescoed, thirteenth-century former chapel, and where the Dominicans have been making lovely scents, tinctures and herbal remedies since the sixteenth century. Also the best pot pourri. Yes, pot pourri.* No, it doesn't have to be vile. There is a tiny branch at 117 Walton Street, London SW3 2HP; tel: 020 7460 6600.

 * I think the only way to prounounce this is the defiant 'pott poo-ry', rather than the à la Française option. I know someone who even says 'Brie' French-style, and it is absolutely grotesque (which she'd pronounce grrrrotesk).

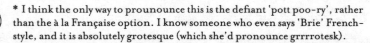

HOW TO HAVE ABSOLUTELY
PERFECT-SEEMING SKIN

You've been paying attention, you've been using the right
products, your skin is looking way better than it has in the past,
and you're happy to do the tinted moisturizer/odd dash of
concealer thing most days. But tonight's a big night and you want
to look *flawless*. This is what you do (it's not quick, by the way — and
not to be attempted anywhere badly lit. Ideally you need one of
those Hollywood starlet mirrors, with bulbs all the way around,
or harsh daylight. Forty watts and a cracked mirror won't do).

1. Moisturize your skin generously, and then go and read a magazine
from cover to cover — we're talking *Heat* rather than the *New Yorker*:
fifteen minutes to half an hour is ideal, a wee bit longer is fine.
If you put your slap on to a just-moisturized face, it'll slide off.
If you put it on dry skin, it'll cake in patches and look weird. You
need the moisturizer to do its thing and to sink in properly.

2. I use make-up artist Laura Mercier's line — she, quite rightly,
has a bee in her bonnet about 'creating perfect skin', and I
heartily recommend her products. If you're using another range
(Estée Lauder does excellent foundations, as do Prescriptives),
look for equivalents.

On your thirst-quenched, moisturized skin, apply a thin layer
of Foundation Primer all over. This is a relatively new product —
all the big names do a version — that may very well be yet another
ingenious way of getting you to part with your money pointlessly.
What it does in theory is create a seal, or barrier, between your
moisturized skin and the slap you're about to pile on top. As I say,
I do see how people might be sceptical about these primers, but
I believe in them. I find they work, provide a smoother base,
protect the skin and make the slap last longer.

3. Get a clean cosmetic sponge, run it under the cold tap and squeeze it as hard as you can so that it is only very, very barely damp. Place two little blobs of foundation on the back of your hand. I use Mercier's oil-free foundation, which is very heavily pigmented, so that you need to use only a titchy amount.* You get what you pay for with foundation. Do ask about pigment concentration when you're buying yours – there's no point in getting a huge, cheap-seeming bottle that needs three clumsy layers to make any difference. It's like buying watercolours when you want acrylics, or indeed oils. Or stucco.

Work the foundation into your skin, using the sponge, and then work it in again, using your fingers. I find the middle fingers are best – they're more sensitive than the gnarled old indexes. When I say work it in, I mean for minutes rather than seconds, and don't forget your eyelids.

4. You now have much nicer skin, but you still have red bits, or the odd broken capillary, or a spot you need to hide. DO NOT slap on more foundation, unless you are deliberately going for the trolley-dolly look, or paying your very own homage to Joan Collins. Get out your concealer. This really should be Laura Mercier's utterly stellar Secret Camouflage (which I owned for years without properly understanding how to use it: ask for a demonstration if you buy it, or for an explanation over the phone). It's expensive, but it lasts for ever (we're back to high levels of pigment), and you could literally hide a port stain with it (though for port stains and their ilk, you might want to try **Dermablend**, available from, among others, **www.escentual.co.uk**). Mix, mix, mix the two colours until you have matched your skin tone perfectly – this takes a bit of practice and will give you something to do on those long winter evenings when you're bored of reading the whole Booker Prize shortlist. Then pat the mix on

 * This is for night-time. In the daytime, for a lunch meeting, say, I use one weeny blob of foundation and a bigger blob of tinted moisturizer, mixed together.

to any problematic areas with the little brush, and pat again with a finger. *Voilà!* Miraculously, the concealer has melded with the base without looking remotely obvious – or indeed detectable. Your skin is now perfectly even – you fox, you – and an immaculate blank canvas. But we're not done yet.

5. You will inevitably have some mixed-up concealer left on the back of your hand. Dip the brush into some eye cream and mix a dot of this with a dot of the concealer, and brush and pat microscopic quantities under the eyes. This feels very nice and fresh, and it gets rid of any shadows (if the shadows are really disastrous, use Touche Éclat as well).

6. You may, at this point, feel that you look a bit matt – a bit too backing singer in Robert Palmer video. Or you may not: it depends on where you're going and what you're planning on doing to the rest of your face. Carry on making up your face and look again when you've finished. If you decide that you'd like a bit of an unmattifying sexy glow, reach for Secret Finish. This is an anodyne-looking white liquid – you squeeze a blob on to your fingers and pat it gently on to your temples, cheekbones and anywhere else you like (go easy, though) for that slightly sheeny, but not iridescent look. It's what they used on Sarah Jessica Parker in *Sex and the City*: it makes your skin look fresh and young and somehow elastic. Whenever I wear this, I get complimented on my amazing, naturally fabulous, glowing skin. And I accept the compliments graciously, chortling to myself. It's a truly great product.

HOW TO LOOK EFFORTLESSLY, CLASSICALLY CHIC, EVEN IF YOU'RE CRAP AT MAKE-UP

Very French, this, and sexy, and fabulous. Also timeless. Wear only red-red lipstick — nothing else. This relies on decent skin and careful application, otherwise you look like Courtney Love or some superannuated Goth leftover.

In order to work, this look requires immaculately groomed and shaped brows: they are *crucial* (see page 20). As is having lips: this doesn't work if you have a slit for a mouth, like a tadpole. If you don't want or don't need to go for the full foundation monty, as described above, just wear tinted moisturizer and concealer where needed — or go bare: all the attention is on your mouth and eyes, not on the odd blemish. You could, I suppose, add a minute slick of mascara, but absolutely nothing else. Works with all colourings and all skin tones, and men *love* it. But get the red right, for heaven's sake — it doesn't work with orange or pink or burgundy. We're talking red-red, as in pillar box, fire engine, sinful apple. Oh, the glamour.

RED LIPSTICKS

Red-red. Orangey-red makes your teeth look beige-brown.
Blue-red only works if you're a glacial blonde. For everyone else,
it's pillar-box red that works best. Try:

- Chanel Rouge Star
- Dior DolceVita
- Yves St Laurent numbers 24 and 40
- MAC Russian Red, Ruby Woo and MAC Red
- Alchemy Devil's Claw
- Nars Jungle Red

I don't believe in lip-liners, so I wouldn't bother with one.
They can look very harsh, and you're after a soft, pulpy red
mouth, not an homage to Cruella deVil.

HOW TO MAKE YOURSELF
LOOK PULLED-TOGETHER IN A HURRY

Light base, as above. Blusher — we're after big, rosy cheeks rather
than stripy carmine streaks. Flat, blunt, thin eyeshadow brush.
Dampen and dip blunt edge into dark — navy, brown, black —
eyeshadow. Open eye; pull up eyelid. Look down. Using brush,
pat the damp shadow *inside* your top lid, from the outside in, from
corner to corner. Less harsh or obvious than kohl or liquid
eyeliner, but makes eye look 'finished' and defined. Mascara.
Vaseline for lips.

WHITER TEETH

Don't smoke, don't drink tea or red wine (hey, why not kill yourself now?) and/or get whitened incredibly expensively by your dentist. Failing that, cheat. Visit www.the-smile-place.com for serious, dentist-quality teeth bleaching, at home. The kit includes the moulding stuff to make your own impressions. You send these back and a dental examiner looks at them and makes a proper mould, as would happen at the dentist. You're then sent the trays back with the peroxide gels for whitening. If you make a hash of taking your mould and the dentist thinks it is not good enough, they will send you more putty stuff to work with free of charge. My dentist charged me about £400 for my bleaching trays; this costs £99 for the whole package. They deliver to Europe and you can buy extra gel applicators separately.

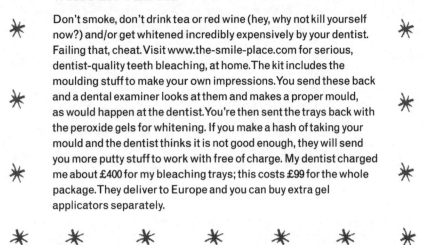

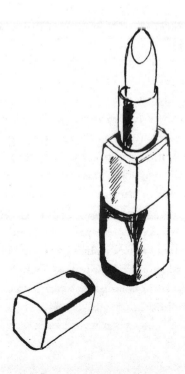

HOW TO MAKE YOURSELF LOOK AT LEAST TEN YEARS OLDER, AND LIKE YOU'VE BEEN ROUND THE BLOCK A FEW TIMES

Ordinary black eyeliner, unsmudged, in two harsh lines, top and bottom. I mean under the lashes, not inside the actual lid, on the bottom. This is a total, total disaster, unless you're in your early twenties, tops, and going for that Gettys in Marrakech look (and even then, this isn't the best way to achieve it). On anyone else — and that probably means you — it is *calamitous*. It's very, very hard, for starters — hard enough to be actively butch (which is why eyeliner worn this way suits most men). And then it closes the eye and makes it look small and avian, like the eye of a horrible mean bird, e.g. a crow, that pecks at corpses. Also, for some reason, even if this and mascara are all you're wearing, you look like you're wearing a ton of make-up: I've lost count of the number of times people have said, 'She wears too much make-up' of some poor woman sporting this hideous look and nothing else. No, unsmudged eyeliner, top and bottom, is a look that reminds me of beefy fifty-year-old prostitutes in Newcastle, with big chins and giant hands. Most women wear it as a matter of course from their thirties onwards, even though it looks horrible and makes them look ancient and birdy. Are they *blind*?

Eyeliner *inside* both top and bottom lids is fine, especially if you have long, almondy eyes. If you don't, I really wouldn't bother: it's not especially flattering. Smudged eyeliner top and bottom is OK, but only if you're deliberately going for the houri look. Smudged top only is good on everyone. Round eyes are good with impeccably applied flicky liquid eyeliner: very *Dolce Vita*. Flicky eyeliner on eyes that aren't round doesn't usually work — it makes them incredibly small. I suppose some people admire Renée Zellwegger's micro-peepers, but I'm not one of them.

MASCARA

If you can afford it, Sisley mascara is the best in the world – long, soft, curved lashes that never look spiky or artificial. Yves Saint Laurent's Mascara Effect Faux Cils is exactly that: makes you look like you're wearing false eyelashes, which means it's not what you'd call a natural look. Brilliant in the evening, though. Max Factor 2000 Calorie mascara is your budget option: fab, but use a lash comb.

Buy some heated eyelash curlers. Yes, they do make a difference, and the newest, battery-operated versions (a selection of which is available from **www.missgroovy.co.uk** — I like the Mr Mascara ones) seem less like a medieval instrument of torture than their predecessors. Failing these, heat old-fashioned curlers with a hair-dryer before applying. Either way, use an eyelash comb, available from all chemists for about a quid. (I can't understand why the eyelash comb isn't a universally used device. All mascaras, no matter how good, cause some clumping, and who needs clumps?)

Obviously, you can't have the lovely face and let it all go to rack and ruin from the neck down. But I don't have any particular recommendations here: I wash with Liz Earle bath wash, or with Dove soap, and, more often than not, wash my hair with the children's cherry-almond-flavoured shampoo, which comes in a pleasing container shaped like a fish. I don't use body lotion, except sometimes on my legs, and have very soft skin none the less, though I say so myself — I think it's because I've never used it in my life, and my skin has adjusted accordingly. Children don't use body lotion, after all, and they have delicious peachy skin. The more I think about it, the more I decide that body lotion, though pleasant enough, is a total swizz. In dermis extremis — wintry elbows emerging in the spring, and so on — you can't go wrong with Palmer's Cocoa Butter: it's cheap, you don't need much and it seems to work overnight.

Hair is a different story. My life has been transformed by finding the right hairdresser: again, this happened very late in my life. I have curly hair, which hairdressers used to love to turn into a sort of big, poodly Afro — they'd stand back, clap their hands with delight and shout, 'Do you *love* it?', as though it were every girl's dream to look exactly like Bruno Martelli from *Fame*. Or they'd make it totally flat and straight, à la Morticia, except with my round face peering out sadly from behind the gloomy black curtains. Then I met Richard, and everything changed. I can't make you meet Richard, alas, but I can encourage you to be *brutal* in your discussions with hairstylists. You need to explain exactly what you want, and to be just as explicit about what you don't. If, mid-cut, you feel alarmed, don't just tell yourself that the stylist knows what s/he's doing and that it's all bound to turn out all right. It isn't. Voice your concerns. Know your limitations, though, and don't be a pain in the arse: if your hair is fine, no stylist is going to give you thick, tumbling locks.

MY BEST HAIRCUT

. . . took place at the Art Luna Salon, 8930 Keith Avenue, Los Angeles; tel: +1 310 247 1383. I appreciate it's not like we all zoom off to LA once a week, but if, for some reason, you should find yourself in this neck of the woods and despair of your hair, come here. They gave me the best haircut of my life: the kind of haircut that completely changed my face, and how I thought of myself. They also do amazing colouring. Celebs ahoy – try not to gawp – but very laid-back and Californian, and the opposite of stuffy. You sit sipping tea in a courtyard while waiting for your stylist.

THE ONLY STRAIGHTENING IRONS WORTH BUYING

. . . are GHD (Good Hair Day) Ceramic Irons – they work miles and miles better than the old-fashioned ones, heat up in seconds and are kinder to your hair, though you still really shouldn't use them too often – and do use them in conjunction with GHD Hair Oil for shine, because without shine, straightened hair looks frighteningly wiggy. Do be slightly careful with straightened hair in the first place, and take it easy: done badly, it is well on its way to becoming the equivalent of the white stiletto. Being skinny, these straighteners also work brilliantly for curling, flicking and so on. Lots of websites sell them, including www.missgroovy.co.uk (fabulous site – hours of fun) and www.edirectory.co.uk, or telephone your order through on 0870 872 0200. Lines are open Mon–Fri, 9–5.30; UK delivery only.

And then there are the other bits. The compelling pop gossip website popbitch (www.popbitch.com) has a fixation with Madonna's supposedly gnarled and aged hands. I haven't had the chance to get a good look, but it is certainly true – and getting gruesomely truer, what with Botox and its ilk – that some women with oddly youthful faces have startlingly unyouthful, claw-like hands. There isn't much you can do about age spots and the like, apart from being zapped by lasers. I've witnessed a friend having a course of these laser treatments – pulse-light therapy, it was called – which seemed to work, but I found the whole process terrifying to watch and wouldn't have it done to myself in a million years.

What you can, and should, do is massage your hands with a nourishing cream (Palmer's Cocoa Butter, as above, is excellent) and either have professional manicures or give yourself them at home. Having said that, some people just have really odd hands – I am thinking particularly of women who have adult-sized hands but with children's tiny, friable fingernails: quite freaky – and all the manicures and polish in the world isn't going to help them.

Pity, really, that gloves aren't more fashionable. But you could always start a trend.

Pedicures are a different thing altogether. They are crucial, and, thank goodness, proper pedicurists are finally appearing in Britain. God knows what took them this long: in Paris, or in Brussels, you can go and have a *pedicure medicale* pretty much anywhere. Given that we're on our feet all day and that we have only one pair, it stands to reason that we should take care of them, by which I do not mean simply painting the toes pretty colours and pushing back the cuticles. I mean serious, heavy-duty stuff that's too unsexy to describe but that leaves you feeling like somebody has very kindly given you new tootsies. Failing an appointment with Mr Gonzales (see box overleaf), do visit your chiropodist: they're not just for old biddies with corns, you know — and anyway, if you get in there early enough, you'll never *be* an old biddy with corns.

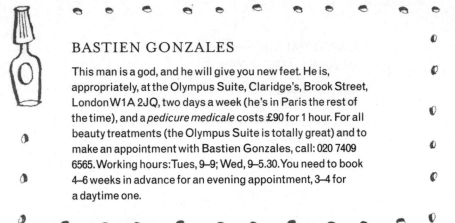

BASTIEN GONZALES

This man is a god, and he will give you new feet. He is, appropriately, at the Olympus Suite, Claridge's, Brook Street, London W1A 2JQ, two days a week (he's in Paris the rest of the time), and a *pedicure medicale* costs £90 for 1 hour. For all beauty treatments (the Olympus Suite is totally great) and to make an appointment with Bastien Gonzales, call: 020 7409 6565. Working hours: Tues, 9–9; Wed, 9–5.30. You need to book 4–6 weeks in advance for an evening appointment, 3–4 for a daytime one.

Working our way back up, we come to the middle bit. Yes, the, um, mons. I know, it's not romantic — and it's not entirely on-subject either. But it's my book, so might I just make a tiny little plea? Having all your pubic hair waxed away is really, really *weird*. By all means, have it tidied up if you are naturally hirsute, or have it topiaried, within reason. But the recent fashion for either a landing strip or having nothing there at all is extremely bizarre. I understand you need to act if you're going to wear a minute bikini, but that kind of waxing still falls within normal realms. What's with having it all off? To put it bluntly, it makes you look like a child. Why would you want your genitals to look like a child's, exactly? Because your boyfriend likes it? Get a new boyfriend, is my advice. Because it makes the area more sensitive? Well, so would tenderizing it with a meat mallet first. I mean, come on. No healthy person's nerve endings are that faulty.

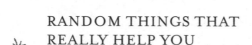

RANDOM THINGS THAT
REALLY HELP YOU

Clarins Beauty Flash Balm Makes the skin look tight. Egg white has the same effect, but is stickier. I am very tempted to insert a quip about sperm here, but shall refrain because of this box's proximity to the pubic plea above. And I am trying to write a classy book (ack! such a foul word, 'classy', like 'cheesy' or 'tasty'). But, er, porn stars tend to have quite good skin.

Issima Midnight Secret by Guerlain. Works miracles: slap it on at night, when you come home at 4 a.m. horrendously the worse for wear and have to do something important at 8 the next morning. Not cheap, but you'll wake up looking like you've had twelve hours' sleep and a facial massage.

Anusol No, it's not an urban myth. If you have massive bags under your eyes and can't afford Midnight Secret, tap on some haemorrhoid cream and they'll nearly disappear. Shrinks piles, *ergo* shrinks skin: stands to reason. But for emergencies only. Interestingly, asking for Anusol at the chemist takes you right back to being twelve (by the way, they like you to pronounce it 'Ahh-noosol', not 'Anus-ole'. I find saying Ahhhnoosol in a public place makes me hysterical and snorty. Anus-ole too, come to think of it.)

Nests

To me, taking pleasure in making lots of effort with one's appearance is the flip-side of taking intense delight in milling about at home, thinking, daydreaming, having frequent naps and not making any effort at all. I couldn't look, or try to look, physically attractive all the time — the very idea makes me feel exhausted. The fact is that dressing/making-up is only really good fun when used as a contrast to lounging about a lot, looking quite pig-like. So this part of the book is all about lounging, which has been my absolutely favourite thing to do since I was a child: some of my happiest hours were spent in bed, with Asterix, later *Jackie* magazine — later still *Honey* — and a bag of Sainsbury's Salt and Vinegar crisps, which came in a chevron-striped blue and yellow packet. I absolutely love bed.

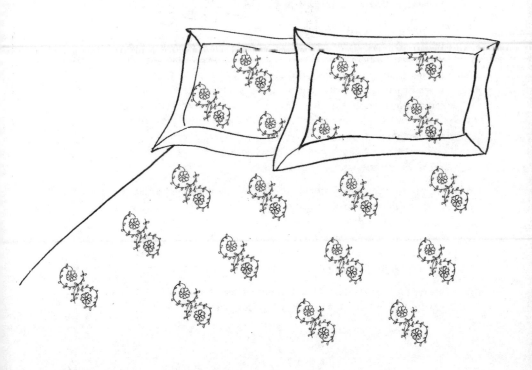

WHAT TO WEAR TO LOUNGE ABOUT AT HOME

Pull-ons – cosy bottoms with elasticated waists that, at a push, you could run to the shops in – from **Boden**, www.boden.co.uk. For inquiries, call: 0845 357 5000, Mon–Sat, 8–8. Worldwide delivery.

The sorts of pyjamas, kaftans and general lounge wear that are very Primrose Hill – boho-chic, at a price, from **Toast**, www.toastbypost.co.uk. For inquiries and catalogue, call: 0870 240 5200, Mon–Fri, 9–8; Sat, 10–6. Worldwide delivery.

Egg 36 Kinnerton Street, London SW1X 8ES; tel: 020 7235 9315. Open: Tues–Sat, 10–6. Lovely textiles for men and women; fine cotton loose-style dresses and tunics from India; also good for fatties. Hugely expensive (OK, rich fatties), but divine, and certainly not only for home wear: these luxurious, understated clothes adorn the best-dressed backs. Skinny backs, too – I feel bad about saying 'rich fatties'. Also beautiful ceramics.

Pickett 32–33 and 41 Burlington Arcade, London W1J 0PZ; tel: 020 7493 8939. Open: Mon–Sat, 9–6. One of my top five favourite shops ever. Leather goods, jewellery and embroidered pashminas so beautiful you could weep. Silk slippers, handbags, not to mention the prettiest backgammon and bridge sets you've ever seen. A must for buying presents, and great for cosy things for yourself: traipsing around with a cold is ameliorated by having a truly beautiful scarf, for example. Browse online at www.pickett.co.uk. For mail-order inquiries and catalogue, call: 020 7626 3636, Mon–Fri, 9–5.30. Will deliver overseas.

Sleepyheads.com Suppliers of cosy, funky pyjamas – printed with, say, milk and cookies, or clouds, or cowgirls – as seen on US sitcoms like *Friends*. Browse and buy online at www.sleepyheads.com; they deliver internationally. If you are located outside the US you may be responsible for duty fees, but this does not happen every time – it seems to depend on the whim of UK Customs.

Harry Duley See page 75. Not lounge wear as such, but incredibly comfy – you more or less forget you're wearing clothes.

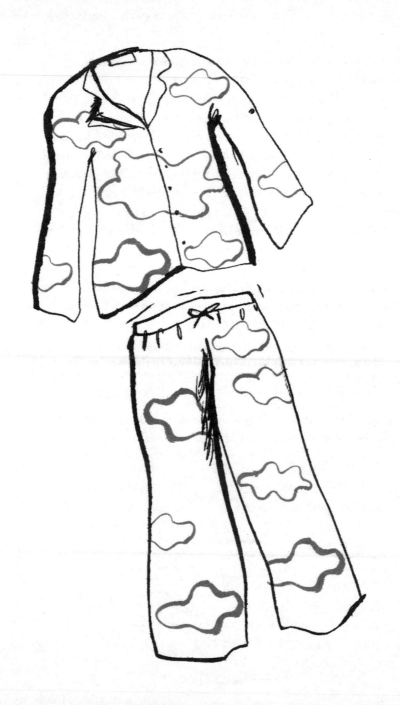

Being naturally indolent to the point of coma, my idea of utter bliss is: fleecy pyjamas, bed, tea, Radio 4 (on Roberts radio), book. Once ensconced, I can keep going for days, and frequently do, receiving visitors in bed and checking the children's homework from beneath my eiderdown. I am blessed — *blessed* — in that I work from home, but I was still pretty damned good at lounging when I worked in offices or shops. I so loved lounging that I used to set my alarm for 7 a.m. on weekend mornings, for the sheer and unbeatable pleasure of waking up thinking 'Oh, no, no, *no*, it's work' and then remembering that, actually, it wasn't, and that I could hunker down again. It's to do with re-creating the feeling of getting ready for school by mistake on the first Monday of half-term: the bliss when you remember that the whole day is yours, to use as you wish, is unforgettable. It's also related to the fact that, once your children sleep through the night, you become obsessed with catching up on your years of sleep deprivation, or at least I do, even though I caught up about five years ago. I also partly blame boarding school: I spent years rising at the crack of dawn and feeling, rightly or wrongly, that I wasn't getting enough sleep. So now, where some women take pleasure in going to the gym, I take utter pleasure in lying down with a book.

The joy of these is not to be believed. Also, I feel very vindicated, because I've had mine for a few years and quite often been asked if I've borrowed my granny's bootees. And then, a few months ago, Uggs started being everywhere: on Pamela Anderson's feet, on Kate Moss's, on Sadie Frost's. Ha! These are Australian sheepskin boots, basically, almost absurdly toasty and cosy — the podal equivalent of a hug. You pull them on and wear them without socks, so you don't get that horrible hot-feet-in-boots thing. The only problem with them is that it's quite hard to go back to normal footwear once the winter is over; also, the bottom part of them is practically round, so that, while they're ideal if you have wide feet, they're not what you'd call elegant. Surprisingly nice with shortish skirts, though, if you have decent legs. They're called Uggs because they ug your calves. I get mine from the wonderful Melvyn at www.aaaaustralia.com, a.k.a. AAA Australia Shopping Mall — and they're called Snugboots, for copyright reasons. They come in natural, chocolate, black and baby pink and you can specify different sorts of sole. Amazingly, if they have your size in stock, the boots arrive 2–4 days after ordering. Just the thing for pottering about at home in — and in the outside world, too. The Celtic Sheepskin Co. is also well worth a look (see page 110).

BED BOOKS

As in things it is particularly blissful to read in bed, as in comfort books – not as in the best books ever written. Naturally they work very well out of bed also but, in the way that fish pie tastes nicer at home than in a restaurant, bed, I feel, is their ideal habitat. My list is kind of obvious, but I pass it on because you may not have read them all, or not re-read them for a while. These are the big beribboned box of violet creams of the book world. (And all my metaphors are food-related: how tragic is that?)

- **Forever Amber**, Kathleen Windsor (Penguin, £8.99). One of my top three all-time faves (Kant, Kristeva, K. Windsor), in or out of bed, but especially well suited for a weekend propped up on pillows, preferably alone, because you'd want to hit anyone who interrupted your reading. Tissues ahoy: the ending is UNBEARABLE.

- Any Georgette Heyer, obviously (Arrow, £5.99). Personal favourites: **Regency Buck** (best title for a novel ever), **The Grand Sophy**, **The Masqueraders**, **Arabella**.

- **The Pursuit of Love**, **Love in a Cold Climate**, **Don't Tell Alfred**, **The Blessing**, Nancy Mitford (all Penguin).

- **I Capture the Castle**, Dodie Smith (Virago, £6.99). Very probably number one comfort-read of all time – and, if not dipped into since adolescence, much darker than you remember it.

- **The Making of a Marchioness**, Frances Hodgson Burnett, (Persephone Books, £10).

- **Miss Pettigrew Lives for a Day**, Winifred Watson (ditto). The sweetest grown-up book in the world.

- **The Cazalet Chronicle** series, Elizabeth Jane Howard (Pan, £6.99).

- **My Cousin Rachel**, Daphne du Maurier – though you have to read it in one sitting, which means 3 a.m., which means *less sleep* (Virago, £6.99).

- **Pride and Prejudice**, natch (Penguin Popular Classics, £1.50).

- Early Jilly Coopers: **Imogen**, **Harriet**, **Octavia**, **Emily**, **Bella** and so on. Sheer bliss. The Sloaney girls! The Sloaney cads! The dogs! (Try second-hand.)

- **Invitation to the Waltz**, Rosamond Lehmann (Virago Modern Classics, £7.99).

- **These Happy Golden Years**, Laura Ingalls Wilder (Avon Books, US, $5.99, or second-hand) and **Anne's House of Dreams**, L. M. Montgomery (second-hand) – like **Little House on the Prairie/Anne of Green Gables**, but the girls are married.

- Any Barbara Pym (Pan, £5.99).

- **Peyton Place**, Grace Metallious (Virago Modern Classics, £7.99).

- **The Real Charlotte**, Somerville and Ross. This and **My Cousin Rachel** are the odd ones out: hardly cosy, but they makes up in bite what they lack in sweetness. I like reading them when I have PMT. The former is out of print, insanely.

I wonder where my love of lounging started. In our flat in Brussels, which was small and empty but perfectly formed, my mother's bed was in the living room, and we spent a lot of time on it (daytime) and in it (mornings, before breakfast). Maybe that's where the bed thing started. Having a bed, though, isn't enough, although I am a great encourager of beds, or bed-like items, scattered about a house. I don't think you can really ever have too many sofas, provided they're squishy, that the cushions are feather not foam, and that there are throws and fleecy blankets for when you feel like being extra-toasty. Besides, people are much more likely to relax and be interesting if they are sitting, or lying, comfortably: you never have much of a laugh when you go to people's houses and they make you sit up straight, on spindly little chairs. Get some beanbags, at least. Argos (the wonder of Argos! See page 124) do excellent ones, cheap — they're crazily over-stuffed, but once you've taken some of the beans out, it's instant comfort, and change from twenty quid. Or spend all your money on giant sheepskin beanbags from the Celtic Sheepskin Co., **www.celtic-sheepskin.co.uk**; **01637 871605**. Utter luxury.

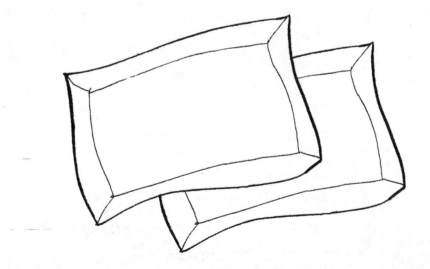

Fine Cell Work This is the most wonderful charity: absolutely beautiful cushions, made, embroidered and appliquéd by prisoners (they also do quilting). The charity was founded by Lady Anne Tree, who, as a prison visitor in the 1960s, became aware of 'how much of the inmates' time was completely wasted . . . Years later, I was determined to try and have an organization in which prisoners could earn money for themselves by learning a top-class skill. Needlework seemed an obvious choice, as it could be worked individually in a cell.' One recent comment about the charity from a resident of HMP Maidstone: 'Anyone can cope with prison physically. It's the mental side that's difficult, so anything that requires you to use your brain is beneficial. Designing the cushions is an achievement.' And from HMP Styal: 'They all come into my room and ask me what I'm doing, and then I teach them embroidery.' And from HMP Wandsworth: 'Perfection is not usually what's expected in prison.'

This is all very lovely and worthwhile, and makes you all warm inside, but it wouldn't be the most terrific amount of cop if the cushions were ugly. Rejoice! They are just beautiful, using the highest-quality materials and embellishing with a degree of skill, craftsmanship and attention to detail that is seldom seen. My cushions – appliquéd pink and green beans on a cream background – are my absolutely favourite thing in the whole living room. Fine Cell Work employs the best teachers, and the quality of their pupils' work is such that it has had commissions from some of England's top interior designers, not renowned for their kind-heartedness, so it's not just me who's impressed. As well as cushions, they make patchwork quilts, embroidered tablecloths, church kneelers, tapestry furniture covers, pincushions and spectacle cases. Cushions from £58; for inquiries, call: 020 8579 1164.

Puppy/Bedstock 26 Portobello Green Arcade, London W10 5TZ; tel: 020 8964 1547. Open: Mon–Fri, 10–6; Sat, 9–6. They do bedlinen, and particularly good cushion covers in two standard sizes; 45 x 45 cm and 65 x 65 cm, though they do also have a limited range in other sizes. If you actually shop at the shop, rather than online, they have a sewing machine on site and can run you up a cover if you have a cushion or bolster that's an awkward or unusual shape. The covers themselves are both camp and kitsch: covered in sushi, or songbirds, or geishas, or the Blessed Virgin looking particularly lovely, rendered in turquoise blue. Also Che Guevara and Mao Tse-tung, cowgirls, cats. Browse and buy online at www.puppy-bedstock.co.uk; worldwide delivery.

THROWS AND BLANKETS

Cath Kidston 8 Clarendon Cross, London W11 4AP; tel: 020 7221 4000. Open: Mon–Fri, 10–6; Sat, 11–6. She does lovely vintage (and faux-vintage) patchwork quilts and 1950s chintzy eiderdowns which are just perfect for snuggling up in front of the telly under. Also fabulous retro rose-strewn wallpaper, cushions, sponge bags, a wee bit of very romantic clothing. Browse and buy a limited selection of the range at www.cathkidston.co.uk. For mail-order catalogue, which carries the full range, call: 020 7229 8000, Mon–Fri, 10–8; Sat, Sun, 10–2.

Melin Tregwynt They do the most beautiful wool blankets, throws and cushions in divine colour combinations and in classic and contemporary designs, including some very funky retro styles (also PJs, nighties and dressing gowns; slippers, hotties, candles and teddies). Browse online at www.melintregwynt.co.uk. For inquiries or to order a catalogue, call: 01348 891 644. These are how you remember blankets being when you were a child, except prettier.

The ideal place to lounge is, of course, the bedroom, which it really is a good idea to turn into a nest. I have only one recommendation bed-wise: Vi-Spring (see box) make the most divine beds known to man. Lying on these is exactly like lying on clouds that are supported by the soft hands of the angelic host. There's no getting away from the fact that they are expensive: I saved up for mine for four years. I used to go into bed shops, lie on my Vi-Spring of choice and sigh with contentment, before having to go home empty-handed to my crappy little back-breaking futon. But Vi-Spring beds are worth every penny. They're like nothing else. They're not beautiful, by the way: you get a sprung base and a mattress, divan-style, and if you fancy

Vi-Spring Luxurious pocket-sprung mattresses with natural fillings. Browse online at www.vi-spring.co.uk. Website lists UK and International stockists. Also available at the London Bedding Company, Selfridges (0870 837 7377), who are very helpful. King-size mattresses (5 ft x 6 ft 6 in) vary from about £1,000 to £4,000 plus. These mattresses were used on the *Titanic* and have been produced since 1901.

Relyon Also pocket-sprung mattresses. Browse online at www.relyon.co.uk. Website lists local retailers. Also available in Harrods and Peter Jones. King-size mattresses vary from around £1,300 to £2,000.

Hypnos Most of their mattresses are pocket-sprung and come in three tensions. Browse online at www.hypnos.ltd.uk. For inquiries, call: 01844 348 200. Stocked in John Lewis, House of Fraser and many more retail stores. King-size mattresses vary from around £500 to £2,300.

a surround you buy it separately. I cannot recommended them highly enough. They've changed the kind of sleep I have. I used to wriggle and squirm and never quite get comfy, and wake up feeling tired even if I'd had twelve hours' sleep. Now I remind myself of my grandmother, who'd get into bed every night sighing with contentment and say, 'This is my favourite time of the day.' (More alarmingly, as soon as she'd get up in the mornings, she'd talk about longing to go back to bed. Either she was depressed or she had a Vi-Spring.) Incidentally, my back isn't great and I'd always subscribed to the theory that this meant I needed a hard bed. This is a myth, it turns out: what I needed was lots of sprung pockets.

So, bed. Fluffy pillows (square as well as rectangular is better for reading). Seriously fluffy duvet that feels like warm whipped cream — nothing wrong with synthetic ones, but if you get everyone you know to donate a fiver towards a Siberian goose-down duvet for your next birthday, you'll know true heaven. A 10.5-tog king-size costs £335 from John Lewis, online at **www.johnlewis.com**: you'll never be cold again, and you feel caressed every time you move. (This would make a wonderful wedding present: not many people spend this kind of money on something as apparently pedestrian as a really fabulous duvet, even though it makes such a difference to one's quality of life.) Fluffy blanket on top for added cosiness rather than warmth. Extras and embellishments as you wish: bolsters, extra cushions, eiderdowns (satin, from Argos, for £25 in baby pink or lilac — I *love* Argos), a bit of fur here or there, to match your boyfriend's chest hair.

For mine, I've also adopted the elements I like best from hotel rooms — the mini-bar, the breakfast tray — and favourites from nursing homes — the handy 'claw', for when you're too lazy to reach for something, the vibrating back massager. I haven't actually invested in anything that would allow me to pee *in situ* — yet — but I've been close, especially as until last year my bedroom was unheated and leaving the warm bed on a December morning was piercing agony.

Browse and buy online from a marvellous selection of titchy fridges and coolers at www.minicoolers.co.uk; they deliver to the UK and Europe. For inquiries, call: 020 8547 3722, Mon–Fri, 9–5.30. You put a carton of milk in, some juice and maybe a box of chocolates and/or jelly beans and, provided you have a kettle in your bedroom, you have your very own version of room service. Good for nail varnish too – it keeps longer – and eye pencils, which stay sharp and hard.

My interest in catalogues featuring goods for the bedridden dates back to my adolescence, I think, when my paternal grandfather, whom I really *loved*, was placed in a home for (probably perfectly valid) reasons which still elude me. It was a very posh home, in Ostend of all places – like a five-star hotel, which is where my nursing home/hotel confusion (I sometimes find it hard to tell them apart) comes from. Anyway, there he was, a bit weak from lung cancer – one lung got shot away in the war, and he smoked eighty Gitanes a day, which does have its heroic side – but otherwise sparklingly compos, bored to death – well, not quite death – by the primped, gossipy old ladies who surrounded him, except when playing chess. You'd go and see him in his room and he'd grab his copy of the paper with a handy mechanical claw to show you something interesting he'd spotted on the op-ed page, and then you'd go down to the dining room and have huge long lunches – always fish – with lots of wine (wine-and-water for me). He died when I was thirteen. An old lady in her eighties appeared at his funeral: it turned out she'd been his mistress for forty years. Nobody would look at her, let alone speak to her. She softly threw some flowers down and then my father took her elbow and ushered her out. I often wonder about her, and about whether she had a family of her own, with or without him. My father wouldn't speak about it, and after the funeral this vexing question was never addressed again, despite my best efforts.

My grandfather left my mother and me all his books: some of them, like a red pigskin-bound Baudelaire which sits on my desk, have messages from the mistress scrawled on the marbled end-papers. She was a defining moment, this old lady. When my grandmother — scandalized, quivering — told me about her later, I remember thinking, 'Good.' Not good for my granny, obviously, but good that my grandpa had somebody who giggled and covered him in kisses and took him to bed. And read books. I'm optimistically assuming she did these things; certainly, my granny — who never quite recovered from marrying 'beneath her' — did not: this much was apparent even to my thirteen-year-old self. I light candles for all three of them when I'm in church. Speaking of which . . .

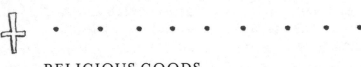

RELIGIOUS GOODS

Graham Kirkland 305 Munster Road, London SW6 6BJ; tel: 020 7381 3195. Open: Mon–Fri, 10–5.30, Sat, 11–4. Dealer in religious art and antiques. Browse online at www.grahamkirkland.co.uk; they will send most goods worldwide. This one really is H.E.A.V.E.N. – silver, statues, vestments, reliquaries, chalices, crucifixes, church chairs, old religious prints – even the odd relic (I once tried to buy a bit of St Euphemia, but someone had beaten me to it). All of it is absolutely beautiful – the shop's constantly changing stock was used in *Harry Potter and the Philosopher's Stone* and in *The Magdalene Sisters*; also in the National Theatre's production of *The Duchess of Malfi*. Fabulous and wonderful.

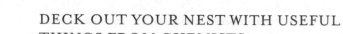

DECK OUT YOUR NEST WITH USEFUL THINGS FROM CHEMISTS

John Bell and Croyden 50–54 Wigmore Street, London W1U 2AU; tel: 020 7935 5555. Open: Mon–Fri, 9–6.30; Sat, 9.30–6. Vast chemist which stocks tools for disabled people as well as stuff from the usual beauty houses, skin care, aromatherapy goods and – at one point, though sadly not at the time of writing – all-natural ribbon-tied condoms made of pig-gut (surefire hit with the lay-deez). Browse online at www.johnbellcroyden.co.uk; worldwide delivery. For inquiries, call 020 7935 5555. Specialist practitioners are also based at the store. Top tips: Helping Hands (the claw), so you don't have to move from your bed when reaching for something; the Long Reach Sponge, for not having to stretch too much while bathing; the Webbed Back Rest, for when you want to sit up and read in bed. Also, the Folding Travel Seat is handy for impromptu fag breaks while walking the dog. But really these are the tips of a giant iceberg – the place is a treasure trove.

Hopefully, the above will have given you a taste for nesting. But with a little ingenuity, the nesting principle can be applied to the whole house: who says you can only loll about in a bed? Not me.

don't want to sound like a fanatical obsessive or loon, but I love my house nearly as much as I love my family. I am really, really attached to it. Not because it's so fabulous that nothing could possibly better it, not because it's smart or grand or fancy (I live in Hackney, east London, there's a crack whore in the flat across the road and my bathroom ceiling's falling down). It's just so *comfortable*, the house, such a haven, and so much a part — an extension — of me, and of all of us who live here, that one of my favourite things about going on holiday is coming home.

I am perplexed by people who don't seem to mind how they live, or what they sit on, or what they look at — in short, I suppose, I am puzzled by (in the cautiously admiring sense) people who don't appear preoccupied in any way by creating a sort of giant nest. I suppose it's to do with how strongly you feel about 'going home', and perhaps it's different if the house in which you grew up still exists, with your parents in it and your trusty Enid Blytons still on the bedside table. But all the houses I grew up in — and there were quite a few — are now lived in by other people, other families, and there's no 'going home' possible: where would I go? I love going to my mother's apartment, but she moved into it relatively recently, and, nice as it is, it is her home, not mine. My father is dead; my stepfather has a lovely house, but it's nothing to do with me. My grandparents, with whom I spent so much time as a child while my mother went to work, are dead too, and their houses were sold long ago. All the significant houses of my childhood are gone, their furnishings and mugs and pillowcases scattered, and I still find this perhaps overly distressing: I've never been back to look at a single one, even when I've been just around the corner from our old London house. In books and films, people are always knocking on the door of their old house and asking to have a look around. I admire this, but can't think of anything worse, by which I mean sadder. Thinking about it, I must have 'issues' with the past: I've never been back to Le Zoute, the seaside town I spent my first eighteen summers in (though I seek out other, similar seaside towns, the greyer the better, like a missile); nor my old schools; nor university. I have quite vivid dreams about some of them, but no conscious thoughts. I've culled them, I guess, though they never did me any harm — *au contraire*.

Anyway, the result is a total nest-making compulsion (I don't think I'm the only one: it seems to me to be very little wonder that people in their thirties, i.e. people with parents who are getting on a bit/have moved to a bungalow, all suddenly get the decorating bug). When I was younger and living in insalubrious student digs, and later insalubrious bedsits, I travelled around like a snail, lugging after me a collection of about sixty postcards of my favourite paintings, some battered cushions, a pair of faded old red velvet curtains and one set of lovely bedding, for comfort and security. I started a heavy-duty decorating process the second I took over the room — paint on the walls, postcards blu-tacked on, curtains at the windows or used as throws, bed made. The advantage of this is that I could feel at home anywhere, very quickly, because I had familiar nest-making materials at my disposal. Which was just as well: what with one thing and another, I lived in a lot of places.

If you feel as I do about going home, and the importance of it, you'll know how marvellous it is to actually create your first home and plonk your family down in it. You sort of feel you've come full circle, except that this time it's going to last *for ever* — a feeling amplified every Christmas, in my case, when we're twenty to lunch and I am blissfully happy and completely unstressed. And yet I still go to people's houses and find them half-empty, unloved, a dying pot plant perched on an ugly fake wood table by a tragic sofa, and I really can't bear it — I actually truly do find it sad. But perhaps these people have very rich internal lives, and no need of external stimulus or comforts.

Perhaps they're too busy having *thoughts* to concern themselves
with the question of finding exactly the right flooring — tough,
child-friendly, aesthetically pleasing, cosy on the toes (rubber
is often what you're after, by the way. Try **Dalsouple, 01278
727 777, www.dalsouple.com** — they can make it up in any
colour you fancy and it can take industrial quantities of abuse,
including projectile vomiting and baby poo. If it's too expensive,
try lino — weirdly unfashionable, but lovely to look at, warm,
tough, now available in pretty colours. Start with a look at
www.forbo-nairn.co.uk. And there's nowt wrong with **cork**,
either — very cheap, very natural, pleasingly squidgy underfoot,
easy on the eye and not deserving of being used only in cheap
bathrooms. You can now get printed cork, featuring pebbles,
grass or big white roses, for instance).

If that's the case, my mind must be a total vacuum, because the
house is packed with things that serve no real purpose outside of
being decorative and making me smile. I am taken aback by those
people who have the kind of kitchens I thought only really existed
in sitcoms: empty, pristine surfaces with one lone kettle sullying
the worktop and no physical evidence (it's all tucked away) that
biscuit-eating, finger-painting, stew-stirring or just nattering
over a cuppa ever takes place. My kitchen is necessarily maximalist,
which means everything is on display, from the finger-paints to
the Jaffa cakes to the thyme growing in a pot for the stew. This
wasn't so much a deliberate look as the result of a cash-flow crisis
when doing the kitchen up some years ago — good old Argos came
to the rescue, with lovely adjustable chrome shelves identical (as
in same manufacturers) to those for sale at a certain shmancy shop
in the King's Road, at, literally, a quarter of the price, i.e. tens of
pounds rather than hundreds — but I'm glad of it now, because
life's too short to go digging about in drawers.

KITCHEN EQUIPMENT

Bloody boring to go and buy, in that it is quite thrilling to purchase but the thrill is spoiled by the fact that it's so often back-breaking and/or awkward to carry home. Do yourself a favour and try the following:

Cucina Direct Excellently stocked. Browse and buy online at www.cucinadirect.com; worldwide delivery, but not of electrical goods or food. For inquiries, call: 020 8246 4311, Mon–Fri, 9–5.

John Lewis Direct Has a good, no-nonsense kitchenware section. Browse and buy online at www.johnlewis.com; UK delivery only. For inquiries, call: 08456 049 049, 7 days a week, 7 a.m.–midnight. For international delivery queries, call: 020 7514 5331.

The Cook's Kitchen Including products from Bodum, Magimix, La Cafetiere, Lazy Fish and De Longi. Browse and buy online at www.kitchenware.co.uk; worldwide delivery. For inquiries, call: 0117 907 0903, Mon–Fri, 10–6.

Lakeland Addictive, and very reasonably priced; huge range of really ingenious things you didn't know you needed. Browse and buy online at www.lakelandlimited.com; worldwide delivery. For inquiries, call: 015394 88100, Mon–Fri, 8–9.30; Sat, 8.30–8.30; Sun, 9–8.30.

Divertimenti 33/34 Marylebone High Street, London W1U 4PT; tel: 020 7935 0689. Open: Mon–Fri, 9.30–6 (Thurs, 7); Sat, 10–6; Sun, 12–5.30. Posh, tasteful, beautiful, professional-quality. Has a section of products especially endorsed by Delia Smith. Browse and buy online at www.divertimenti.co.uk; worldwide delivery.

Cookcraft Part of the Aga group. Browse and buy online at www.cookcraft.com; worldwide delivery. For inquiries, call: 01952 642000, Mon–Fri, 9–5, and ask for Cookware Dept.

Beststuff.co.uk Absolutely terrific, if basic-looking, site that sells, among other things, kitchen equipment – but also computer stuff, TVs, cameras, phones, stereos and so on – all kinds of electrical goods, basically. The idea is that many sites just have too much on offer and that the whole shopping process becomes bewildering for the shopper. They've done the work for you: they sell only things that they believe to be the best in their category – so for instance, if you want a blender, you can pick from three: the best expensive blender, the best mid-range blender and the best cheap blender, along with explanations of why they're the best. Browse and buy online at www.beststuff.co.uk; prompt delivery to anywhere in the UK is, unusually, included in the price. For inquiries, call: 01926 647 882, Mon–Fri, 9–5.30.

Thecookingshop.com This has a more aesthetically pleasing collection than most, including Nigella Lawson's beautifully designed (with Sebastian Conran) range. If you thought you'd never buy anything that came with a 'celebrity' endorsement, think again.

IN PRAISE OF ARGOS

Where do I begin? Or, more to the point, where do you? That's the thing about Argos: rather like shopping at C&A when it still existed, you have to plough through a lot of rubbish to find the goodness, but when you do, you end up with utter jewels. I've already mentioned the fabulous satin eiderdowns, the plain cream beanbags, the smart wire shelving of the kind you find in French groceries or expensive Notting Hill delis, but every new catalogue offers up a fresh batch of treasures. You have to take the catalogue home — it doesn't do to carry out this kind of shopping in a hurry — and browse at your leisure. Plough past the salmon-coloured sofas, the gold-edged ceiling lights, the dolls that pee, the dodgy jewellery (excellent earrings, though, should you be in a ghetto-fabulous kind of a mood) and instead feast your eyes on the bedding, the kitchen equipment (same toasters as Harrods, half the price), the modernist halogen lamps, the impeccably ripped-off Christine Keeler chairs . . . I'm not going to give any more specific examples, because, as I say, the catalogue's contents change all the time, but please do check them out. There are absolute marvels in there, at rock-bottom prices — maybe not hundreds and hundreds of them, but certainly dozens. People are sniffy about Argos and I can't understand why. I think it's fantastic.

This nest-building, or womb-fixation, as some might see it, extends, naturally, to the bath. I don't love baths for being refreshing; rather, I see them as yet another marvellous place to rest and daydream in. I have incredibly cheap bathroom suites in my house – I think they cost under £300 each (cheap suite, painted tongue-and-groove all around: looks marvellous, costs a pittance) – and the bathrooms themselves are absolutely titchy, but I still adore them. Actually, I have a hate thing about flash bathrooms, I don't know why. I fell off a bathroom table when I was a baby – maybe I harbour some terrible resentment. Certainly, I despise flashy bathroom taps – which reminds me: do consider installing **hospital taps** in bathrooms. They have long 'ears', like rabbits, and you can turn them on and off with your elbow. Very useful if you're carrying a baby in one hand and balancing nappies and wipes in the other.

The crucial thing about baths is to have *absolutely delicious* bath products. Sodium laureth sulphate, a sinister chemical, is often to be found in bath products and in 90 per cent of shampoos. I say sinister because it is a component of antifreeze and is, according to some, carcinogenic. It's in a lot of things – it makes bubbles and foam happen – and I've only recently realized that this is the thing that makes my sensitive skin flare up: there's nothing worse than a weekend away being ruined by soaking myself in some nice hotel's unlovely, though undeniably deluxe, bath products. I'd avoid it. Even if it's actively good for you – which I most sincerely doubt: there's an excellent case to be made for having it banned – it irritates the hell out of sensitive skin, including that on your scalp. See box overleaf for bath products that don't contain any SLS and work on even the most rash-prone of us.

BATH PRODUCTS FOR SENSITIVE SKIN

Presumably I don't have to direct you to your local health shop.
For less obviously wholesome, sandally things, see Dr Hauschka,
page 80. Personally, I am devoted to REN, skincare products that
use 100 per cent natural ingredients – the bath oil and body wash
in Moroccan Rose Otto are transportingly lovely and you only need
to use a titchy amount; shampoos also. Browse and buy online at
www.ren.ltd.uk; they deliver worldwide. For inquiries, call: 0845 22
55 600, Mon–Fri, 10–4. Their flagship store, at 40 Liverpool Street,
London EC2M 7QN; tel: 0207 618 5353, is open Mon–Fri, 11–7.

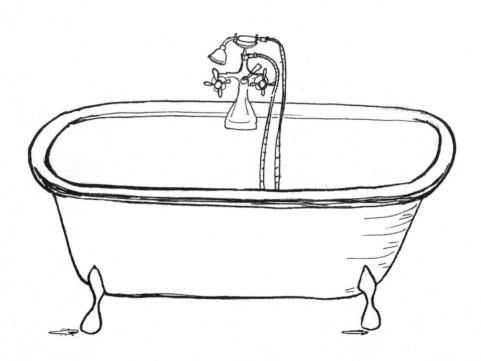

All this sleep, all these baths . . . at some stage, a person needs to get some work done. As I've already said, I work from home. So does my boyfriend, which is potentially fatally distracting. We didn't know what to do when he moved in: whether one of us should rent an office, or build an extension, or whether we should move house (aaargh).

And then the solution came: **a shed in the garden**. And not just any old shed either – a beautiful, weatherboard-clad mini-house that looks like something from New England. It is entirely aesthetically pleasing, has its own tiny veranda, and is big enough internally (10 ft x 12 ft, but they come in every size) to fit a desk, shelving, an armchair, a smaller spare desk and a rug. It is absolutely lovely and I am very jealous of it. Also, there is an especial pleasure in just taking a few steps down the garden to go to work, especially when it's pelting outside – just think of the cosiness. The shed (moss green on the outside, baby yellow on the inside, with a pitched roof) is from www.garden-studios.com, 01949 860 482, who are a delight to deal with and whose designs are as attractive as they are efficient. The most marvellous thing of all is that your shed arrives on a giant crane, the roads are closed off and it is dropped into place – the experience is reminiscent of Dorothy's house whizzing about through the air in *The Wizard of Oz*. Prices start from about £10,000 – not, I think, insanely expensive for a whole new room (and sheds can be anything: offices, playrooms, guest rooms, even – they have light, heating, phone sockets, the lot) and considerably cheaper than moving house. And you can take it with you when you leave, should you choose to.

OFFICE SUPPLIES

Viking Direct Get everything you might conceivably need for your home office delivered to your door. Browse and buy online at www.viking-direct.co.uk. For inquiries or a catalogue, call: 0800 424 444, Mon–Fri, 8–8; Sat, 8–4; Sun, 10–4. They're very friendly. Small delivery fee if goods come to under £30, free otherwise. If you place your order by noon, it'll arrive later that day 99 per cent of the time unless you live somewhere very remote; otherwise next-day delivery.

abc-inkjets.co.uk Like it says: bloody ink cartridges for your bloody printer. Don't know about yours, but mine is a nightmare and permanently on the blink. For inquiries, call: 07000 438 739.

See also Manufactum (see page 136) – their office section is excellent and would make any desk look lovely, in a retro, non-frivolous, Busy Beaver kind of way.

It can become quite obsessive, shopping for the home. We've all been there: you think, 'I really can't afford that beaten-up 1930s leather sofa, and I don't actually *need* it, but on the other hand I know, with blinding certainty, that if I *did* buy it, my life would change 100 per cent for the better.' This is the conundrum at the heart of shopping. Some might argue, perfectly reasonably, that all the sofa is going to change is the already parlous state of your bank balance. Others might say, truthfully, that the need to acquire superfluous *stuff* in this way isn't healthy, and probably speaks volumes about self-indulgence and denial. These are both valid, if over-ploddy and over-pragmatic, responses. Taken to its extreme conclusion – the stuffed carrier bags and unopened boxes crammed with booty that sit under the beds of more miserably married women than you'd care to imagine – the shopping compulsion does indeed begin to look like an illness. It is, after all, easier to blow £300 in John Lewis than it is to tell

your husband that your marriage is over, just as it is easier, for
some people, to eat a whole cheesecake after an argument than
to admit to feeling incredibly upset and hurt. Well, easier in
the short term, at any rate.

But this is not the sort of shopping I am describing. There is a
difference between the wilder manifestations of retail therapy – so
called, presumably, because what you're actually doing in therapy
terms is 'making me-time' – and simply feeling happy that you
have a new sofa to park your bottom on. The difference isn't huge,
except in one respect: shopping born of unhappiness serves to
obscure, and shopping born of joy to . . . well, illuminate, really.
If I am feeling ecstatically happy and want to go and buy armfuls
of flowers as a result, I will feel even happier sitting in my house,
sniffing the air and letting my eye rest on bowls and bowls of lovely
fat old-fashioned roses. I won't feel happier because I am a
repulsive capitalist monster, urged on by greed and the need to
acquire and amass, nor because buying flowers is some sort of
displacement activity that covers up the fact that the foundations
of my happiness are built on sand. Buying the flowers is, surely,
nothing better or worse than an act of joy, an impulse springing
from delight, unless you're Mrs Dalloway (for whom the buying
of flowers is a prelude to packing it all in – but then, whoever said
V. Woolf was made for the world of the cheery?).

FLORIST

I use only one florist, because, having tried dozens over the years, they're the best. This is very unhelpful to you if you don't live in London – apologies. But the flowers that Harper and Tom's put together are so achingly beautiful that I just had to include them. They are the opposite of 'done' flowers, and very much bunches rather than bouquets. Last Mother's Day, for instance, I sent my mum a huge armful of lilacs. It's a question of personal taste: if you like stiff arrangements with quirky twigs and ornamental grasses, you won't like these flowers. I love them. It is as though they stock their blooms from an overgrown cottage garden. Also, unusually for London, you get a lot of flower for your quid. Their shop, at 73 Clarendon Road, London W11 4JF; tel: 020 7792 8510, is open Mon–Fri, 9–6. London deliveries only.

If you're sending flowers to someone anywhere in Britain and don't want to be reliant on Interflora, please have a look at www.jwflowers.com and www.foreverflowering.com, both of whom send out wonderful vivid bunches that couldn't be further removed from the usual carnation 'n' gyp.

What, then, of the sofa? It's the same thing, I think – assuming you haven't got a warehouse somewhere stuffed with ninety-nine more. From flowers to sofas to hair bobbles to especially pleasing Bic lighters, the kind of shopping I am describing is life-enhancing. The fact of the matter is that buying the big 1930s leather sofa *will* make your life better, because you'll feel a little surge of joy every time you walk past it or sit on it. It won't *change* your life, in that it won't give you a new boyfriend or a bigger bust. But if it is purchased with reasonably realistic expectations, it is more than

likely to fulfil them. Surges of joy are worthwhile things; without
them, life would hardly seem worth bothering with.

Digression over. I had to get it off my chest, because people misunderstand shopping so (though I can see how it happens: Victoria Beckham, laden with bags, tottering down Bond Street daily on her sparrow legs, turns even my stomach. Shopping has such bad role models). And of course you could argue that people who claim to despise shopping are despising themselves: taking no care with their surroundings, not caring what they put in their mouths, or their children's, not caring what they look like, or at. I wouldn't dream of being so unkind as to point this out to them, which is why I wish a certain kind of person wouldn't snigger defensively at women who like buying eyeshadow (that's another thing: I can't bear the snobbery involved when it comes to judging the act of shopping. Shopping for shoes makes you an air-headed prat; shopping for first editions gives you gravitas. Why? Both the shoe fiend and the book collector are pursuing private passions. Who's to say which is 'better' or more inoffensive?).

Anyway, this leads me quite neatly to the question of money. Shop haters and non-admirers of shopping are always vocal about the grotesqueness of spending money – 'good money', usually – on frivolous things like, um, chairs or loo paper (Kleenex Quilted Velvet. Why should you scrape away at your bottom with hard, crispy paper?). The idea that shopping necessarily involves monstrous quantities of ready cash is nonsense; as is the idea that shopping is essentially a middle-class pursuit. Middle-class families don't go for days out at Bluewater or Brent Cross; middle-class families don't go out on Saturday afternoons with the sole intention of spending their cash; and the queues at Peter Jones are nothing to the frenzied omni-chaos of Argos. So enough of this rubbish: shopping is only elitist if you're Michael Jackson checking out some urns, or a too-brown anorexic lady-who-lunches weighed down with Rolexes. Which cuts out 99.9 per cent of the population, thank heavens.

ON THE CHEAP

We all love bargains, in theory at least. In practice, bargain-hunting most often means hitting the sales, which I personally can't be doing with. Basically, at the sales, you're buying the stuff no one else wanted – you're doing the store a huge favour by getting past-it, otherwise unshiftable stock off their hands, and paying for the privilege. Aside from the odd giant reduction – I can see the point of waiting for the sales to buy a new stereo or hugely reduced American-style fridge – this is a complete waste of time. You end up with something 'cheap' that you didn't actually very much either want or need; it would have been cheaper, and more of a bargain, frankly, not to have bought it in the first place.

This isn't to say that bargains don't exist. Outside of sales, they are everywhere. The trick – and the pleasure – is to look in improbable places. I've already mentioned Argos, which is a veritable treasure trove for the bargain-hungry. My personal favourites are high-street hardware shops, such as Robert Dyas. It used to be that, as it were, the Conran Shop – which I am using as shorthand for any kind of designer emporium – was king when it came to desirable things for your home, but this is no longer true. The kind of gleamingly chrome-y kitchen equipment – retro-modern toasters, kettles, pots, pans, spoons, ladles, tongs and so on – that used to be found only in poncy and expensive shops, artfully displayed surrounded by scattered petals and/or some interesting grasses, are all mass-manufactured and now available from your local high street. Tea towels are an especial forte of old-fashioned hardware shops, I find: plain linen with blue borders, three for a fiver, and so beautiful and evocative that you practically want to wear them.

There are bargains to be had for every room in the house. Paint colours that were hitherto only available to people who lived in Fulham are now available to all, at a fraction of the original prices – including 'historic', which is to say ointment-coloured, ranges, which I personally find somewhat bewildering: who wants to paint the sitting room of their tiny terraced house in a colour called 'Chatsworth'? Still, there's democracy for you. Far more interesting to my mind are the colour-matching services offered by Dulux, among others: you take along a scrap of your favourite fabric, or an old photograph, or whatever, and they come up with a paint that matches its colour exactly (which is how, in a fit of over-enthusiasm, I came to have, for a time, walls which were the perfect orange of an Hermès box. I don't know why I'm having a go at 'Chatsworth', really – this is even worse). If you were terribly sneaky, you'd spend £3 on a swatch from John Oliver – 33 Pembridge Road, London W11 3HG; tel: 020 7727 3735, to my mind the shop with the finest range of paint colours – and, well, rip them off via your friendly Dulux consultant.

I don't know why it should be so difficult to find attractive, reasonably priced lighting in this country, but it is: cheap lamps are a nightmare. However, BhS has an excellent lighting department if you look for long enough, as do Debenhams: the interiors diffusion line by John Rocha is particularly worth checking out if you have only (only! – you see what I mean about lighting being so expensive?) £75 to spend on a standard lamp.

Actually, all the interiors diffusion lines at Debenhams – Designers at Debenhams, it's called – are worth checking out. Annoyingly, they don't do Cath Kidston's 1950s-inspired chintz-meets-gingham line any more, but IKEA has stepped into the breach with its brilliant, dirt-cheap rip-offs: the prettiest retro-chintzy duvet covers ever – apart from the real thing, of course – for £10 for a single; also cushions; also sofas. I know shopping at IKEA is a nightmare – though I am oddly fond of the Swedish meatballs to be had in its cafeterias; I find these soften the blow somewhat – but it's worth it. The trick is not to get overwhelmed by the cheapness of things and therefore start piling your trolley high with stuff you don't need, but rather to pace the floors stealthily and pick up a few really good things. Again, the kitchenware department is particularly impressive, but the textiles are great too, and I've bought some terrific, huge, plain wool rugs in boiled-sweet colours there – these being the rugs that get compliments whenever anyone sees them. The sofas are terrific, too – the catalogue at the time of writing has, in particular, pea-green corduroy sofas and fat rose-strewn ones at really rock-bottom prices: why bother going elsewhere when you could get one of each for the price of a standard three-seater from somewhere supposedly smarter?

Three things that are never worth economizing on: coffee, butter, loo paper.

KARAOKE

What better way of watching the pennies than by making your own entertainment? Karaoke is such a laugh. I'm not naturally exhibitionistic, and nothing, short of being forced to down a bottle of tequila in one, would ever induce me to sing karaoke in public, in front of total strangers — partly because I'm shy and partly because I truly can't sing (as opposed to those people who say, 'Oh, no, I'm practically tone deaf' and turn out to be Sarah bloody Brightman). But having a karaoke machine in your own living room is another thing altogether — it is just the best fun. What is anthropologically fascinating about it is that it's always the quiet ones — the ones who say 'I couldn't possibly' and look appalled by the very idea — who go on to hog the mike for two hours and have to have taxis ordered for them at 3 a.m. The karaoke machine is fun if there's only two of you and a bottle of wine, fun if there's twelve of you, fun if there are children around, marvellous for family gatherings, and absolutely a must for any large party. The thing that people don't realize is that you can get karaoke CDs of absolutely everybody: it doesn't all have to be chart bands, soap stars or old standards. We have masses of Gershwin and Cole Porter in among the 1980s classics, lots of country and western, Billie and Ella, old Irish songs — even a particular favourite called **Karaoke Punk**, which, tragically, holds enormous appeal for men of around forty . . . Basically, if it's ever been recorded, it's on a karaoke CD and you'll be able to buy it online from hundreds of sites, too numerous to list here, both in the UK and in the US. The crucial thing is to look for the letters CDG or CD+G on the CD — this stands for CD + graphics, and of course it's the graphics — the lyrics — that you want to sing along to on your TV screen. CDs that don't feature these letters expect you to squint at the tiny print of the CD leaflet for lyrics, which is hopeless.

*Now the machine: there is no point in going mad and spending a
fortune, at least not initially. There are three kinds of machines. First,
the ones that plug straight into your TV, using this as a screen to read
the lyrics off — fine if your TV is somewhere accessible like the middle of
the living room. Or you can get little machines with a small TV screen
built in, so that you literally plug the machine in anywhere and go. And
then there are the fancier arrangements, which also work on principle
B but are much more powerful (and expensive — though sometimes
£100 makes all the difference). The only thing to watch out for with
the smaller machines is that they need to have enough power to be
sufficiently loud. You really need a specialist shop to buy a proper
karaoke machine — everything the high street sells is, in this instance,
crap. Have a look at www.emkaraoke.co.uk, which is a chaotic-
looking but friendly site from which I got my machines (also
0115 924 5454; great advice over the phone).*

Having said all of that about bargains, some things just
ain't cheap and some things you just have to pay for (like proper
scented candles that actually smell of something for longer
than three minutes*). My very favourite interiors shops follow —
and not a bargain to be had between them.

* Try those by Diptyque (whose shop is due to open in Westbourne Grove,
London WII, shortly) and Jo Malone (150 Sloane Street, London SWIW 9BX;
tel: 020 7730 2100, Mon–Sat, 9–6). These burn longer and are packed
with scent, showing up cheap candles that burn down to nothing in an hour
for the total swizz they really are. Laura Mercier also does a nice one that
smells exactly like there's a lemon tart in the oven.

BEST INTERIORS

David Champion 199 Westbourne Grove, London W11 2 SB; tel: 020 7727 6016. Open: Tues–Sat, 10–6. Beautiful, beautiful things and objects, from emu eggs and ornate birdcages to French leather chairs and porcupine quills. The stock changes constantly, so you really need to go and have a look.

Tann-Rokka 123 Regent's Park Road, London NW1 8 BE; tel: 020 7722 3999. Open: 7 days a week, 10–6. Contemporary and antique things, all beautiful, all with an Eastern bent. Mirrors, lamps, tables – and, oddly enough, their own very delicious scent, Kisu. Charming service.

Labour and Wait 18 Cheshire Street, London E2 6 EH; tel: 020 7729 6253. Open: Sat, 1–5; Sun, 10–5; Fridays by appointment. Old-fashioned and beautiful hardware shop selling old-fashioned, beautiful and useful household goods: little enamelled pans in lovely colours, colanders, brooms.

Manufactum Ltd Lovely catalogue – very stylish, classic, robust kitchenware, lighting, furniture, leather goods, office stuff, toys (wonderful) and clothing (very German). Browse and buy online at www.manufactum.co.uk (.com for international). For inquiries; call: 0800 096 0938, Mon–Fri, 8–8; Sat, 8–2.

Cabbages and Roses 3 Langton Street, London SW10 0JL; tel: 020 7352 7333. Open: Mon–Sat, 9.30–5.30. Hand-printed linen, cotton and muslin bedding, cushions, oilcloth, fabric to recover your sofa with. Just beautiful. Also skirts, dresses, bedwear. Browse online at www.cabbagesandroses.com; worldwide delivery. For inquiries, call: 01225 859151.

Interiors magazines are always going on about how your garden
is really an extra room. After years of forcing myself to learn,
I am now a reasonably competent gardener, which is to say that
things have stopped dying the minute I look at them. I am all for
the garden-as-room theory, though. Our ultra-minute Lond
on garden – there's a large shed in it, remember – became much
nicer when I got rid of its grass (spoken like a true nature lover,
I know). This isn't a course of action I would recommend to
anyone with a garden of any real size, but if your garden is small,
you could do far worse than plant the borders, let the trees be and
pave the rest. It saves so much hassle. If you string fairy lights from
tree to tree in the summer and haul out old throws and cushions,
you get an almost instant casbah-effect that is very pleasing,
and you don't need to faff about with (and find storage for)
lawnmowers. If you have a dog in town, incidentally, this seems
to be the only reasonable course of action: dog shit and small
town gardens really don't go together. And you can chuck
a bucket of bleachy hot water over paving stones.

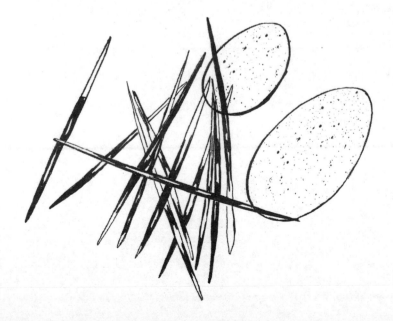

DOG THINGS

Classy Pets Boutique Excructiatingly bad name, fabulous contents: the best deluxe collars, many featuring elaborate quantities of diamanté, but also leather flowers, beading and so on and glitzily on. Lots of pink; positively decadent dog beds. Not what you'd adorn your gun dog with, but anyone with the slightest Liberace tendencies will be in heaven after a visit to this site. Also cats' stuff. Browse and buy online at www.classypets.com; they ship worldwide. For info, e-mail: info@classypets.com.

Dogmcuk.com Bonkers doggy fashion with an English accent: football strips, Hairy Potter outfits – completely eccentric. Browse and buy online at www.dogmcuk.com; they deliver worldwide. For inquiries, call: 020 7778 8220, Mon–Sat, 9–5.30. Very friendly.

Bluepet Sells sometimes hard to find organic cat and dog food, including Nutro, and delivers to your door within two days. Also collars, leads, beds, toys, natural remedies. Browse and buy online at www.bluepet.co.uk; worldwide delivery. For inquiries, call: 0845 330 6451, Mon–Fri, 9.30–4.30.

Pet 351 Archway Road, London N6 5AA; tel: 020 8341 4888. Open: Mon–Fri, 10–7; Sat, 10–5; Sun, 11–3. More organic pet food and recherché, well-sourced accessories and toys. Very beautiful shop and contents: like Barneys for creatures. Goods can be posted to you; call for details.

NURSERIES/BULBS AND SEEDS

Architectural Plants Nuthurst, Horsham, West Sussex
RH13 6LH; tel: 01403 891772. Open: Mon–Sat, 9–5. Evergreens,
exotics. Browse online at www.architecturalplants.com – an
excellent site; mainland UK delivery. There is also a second
nursery in Chichester – details on the website. Do get them
to send you one of their lovely, witty, fascinating catalogues.

Peter Nyssen Ltd 124 Flixton Road, Urmston, Manchester
M41 5 BG; tel: 0161 747 4000. Open: Mon–Fri, 9–5. Indoor and outdoor
bulbs by mail order. Wonderful baroque names for colours. Browse
and buy online at www.peternyssenltd.co.uk; EU delivery.

Crocus For plants, climbers, small trees, garden accessories.
Browse and buy online at www.crocus.co.uk; mainland UK delivery.
For inquiries, call: 0870 000 1057, 7 days a week, 24 hours a day. They
also provide a garden maintenance service for parts of the London
area and the Home Counties; call for details. Website is cheery and
comprehensive.

Sarah Raven's Cutting Garden Gardening's equivalent
of The Cross. Supplies a huge variety of seeds, from perennial
and biennial flower seeds to vegetable, herb and salad seeds,
plus all you need to create a meadow. Browse and buy online at
www.thecuttinggarden.com; will deliver overseas. For inquiries,
call: 01424 838181, Mon–Fri, 9–5. Also supplies garden and flower
arranging kits, gift packs, books and tools.

Classic Roses – The Peter Beales Collection Stocks more
than 1,300 roses. Browse and buy online at www.classicroses.co.uk;
worldwide delivery (a few exceptions). For inquiries, call:
01953 454707, Mon–Sat, 9–5; Sun, 10–4. Roses can be found by
provenance, colour, alphabetically or by families and height. A
search finder also allows you to select a rose by type of scent, time
of flower and suitability to your garden. There is a free telephone
line just for advice on roses: 0800 169 2259, Mon–Fri, 9–4.30.
Utterly wonderful.

I pined for a trampoline for ages and this year I finally bought one for the house we currently rent in the country. It is huge — up to three adults can comfortably bounce at the same time. It's the best outside thing I've ever bought, the trampoline. Children come to stay, bounce themselves into a stupor and then collapse into a coma-like sleep until at least 10 a.m., which is ideal behaviour in a child-guest, I feel. Adults — well, it's a test of character: some are too shy, but can't resist and then go and have a secret bounce at night; some are show-offs and immediately attempt the wilder moves, like backwards somersaults; some just bounce and bounce, going 'wheeee' and making you love them. Also, trampolining constitutes excellent aerobic exercise: ten minutes trampolining burns as many calories as half an hour's jogging (and is a lot more fun), so you're getting a workout at the same time as arsing around going 'boing'. Mine is from the sexily named Supertramp, **www.supertramp.co.uk, 0800 197 1897** — not cheap, though. You can get trampolines at bargain-basement prices elsewhere on the net; do use your head before buying these. Find out about the springs and structures and metals and guarantees before you buy: some cheap trampolines are so feebly constructed that they are potentially extremely dangerous, especially when used by boisterous, semi-hysterical children. If in doubt, rent ('If in doubt, make it third,' my Latin teacher used to say when we didn't know which declension to use) — check your local *Yellow Pages*. Small note of warning: trampolines are irresistible to drunk people, and this usually leads to a trip to Casualty. If you're going to get drunk, lock the doors and ban bouncing.

The only other thing I really pine for in my garden is my very own public house. I don't think it's ever going to happen, though I live in hope.

A MINI-PUB!

Keenmac Pubs supply these, in several sizes from micro to maxi, artfully themed – trad, Irish, 1950s Americana, Victorian, etc. etc. etc. (there are more options than you could believe). They are proper working pubs, with optics and bars, and feature all the accoutrements you'd expect, from 'shelf bric-à-brac' to name boards, display cases, mirrors and so on. Amazingly brilliant – and if you live in the middle of nowhere, a marvellous antidote to dodging the drunk drivers or being one yourself. Browse online (feast your eyes) at www.keenmacpubs.com. For inquiries, call: 028 4063 1530, Mon–Fri, 8–5.30. They're based in Northern Ireland but can deliver worldwide, and each pub and its contents are 'tailored to the individual'. What more could anyone want?

I think renting a house/cottage somewhere is better, with children, than booking a hotel – you may end up playing the cleaner as well as the cook and chief washer-upper, but at least the children can run around in peace and safety without getting in anyone's way.

In Britain, my experience is that **Rural Retreats** (www.ruralretreats.co.uk, 01386 701177) provide a uniformly very high standard of accommodation, from their small cottages to their grander mansions, and from Gloucestershire to the Scottish Highlands. There are nice little touches, like a basket of essentials waiting for you on the kitchen table so that you don't immediately have to race out to the nearest grocer's; in some of the properties, it is possible to arrange for home-made food to be delivered. The houses are, as a rule, un-nattily decorated and, more importantly, pristine; a number of them accept dogs.

In the Cotswolds, **Bruern Stable Cottages** (www.bruern.co.uk) provide ten absolutely idyllic cottages on the Bruern estate. The cottages sleep two to eight and each is really beautifully and opulently appointed, and lovely-looking – we're talking antiques, open fires, blissfully comfy beds and no expense spared; you can even specify whether you'd prefer down duvets, or synthetic, or allergy-tested, or blankets. You can also arrange to have the fridge/freezer stocked with a selection of yummy home-cooked meals for when you arrive; papers and milk are delivered daily. There's a swimming pool and tennis court for the summer, kids' toys in the large communal garden (each cottage also has its own, smaller garden or orchard, complete with barbecue and big white umbrella), a lovely children's playhouse and a giant doll's house. Deluxe in an understated and very English way: not at all the place for a raucous hen weekend, but absolutely heavenly for a week's gentle holiday en famille (or as a minibreak present for your parents/best friends. One of the cottages that sleeps two is incredibly romantic). Very nesty.

Try also the **National Trust** and the **Landmark Trust**, both of which provide spectacular properties in often spectacular locations (you need to book months ahead for some), though comfort and nesting aids are not necessarily the first priorities here: the properties are listed and, obviously, in trust, so their keepers can hardly go about scattering fleecy blankets and useful ashtrays. This does mean that some of the bigger houses can be bracingly spartan (but never actively uncomfortable). The Landmark Trust has some lovely lighthouses in addition to the more traditional places.

Abroad: wonderful houses in Ireland – a brilliant place to go on holiday, not least because even the pubs are almost ludicrously child-friendly, and taking the ferry is old-fashioned fun – from the unpromisingly named but extremely helpful and friendly **www.tourismresources.ie** at 71 Waterloo Road, Dublin 4; tel: +35 31 478 2045.

Italy: villa specialists Italian Chapters (also French Chapters, Greek Chapters, Moroccan, Croatian, etc. etc.) now come under the **Abercrombie & Kent** umbrella. Brochures and information from www.abercrombiekent.co.uk; tel: 0845 070 0610. This is an upmarket company with prices to match, but the houses are fabulous and prices drop if you decide against Chiantishire or the old South of France (I am particularly fond of northern France: Brittany is, in its way, as fabulous as the south, much, much cheaper, and the beaches are beautiful). Try also **Veronica Tomasso Cotgrove**, 10 St Mark's Crescent, London NW1 7TS; tel: 020 7267 2423 (www.vtcitaly.com), who has some lovely properties in, natch, Tuscany, the Marche and Capri. She also has some beautiful apartments in La Serenissima – but for heaven's sake don't go to Venice in the summer; it is especially magical in the winter and early spring, and the crowds much more manageable.

Elsewhere: **Best of Morocco**, admirably run by Chris Lawrence, are a joy to deal with and have some absolutely wonderful properties which you can take over, also riads (like B&Bs, but spectacular) and small, sexy hotels that are the opposite of soulless. They really know their stuff, and it needn't cost a fortune. Yes, you do get hassled in Morocco, but going with children cuts this down by about 80 per cent – as does dressing modestly (obvious, but true. It's a Muslim country: don't wear micro-shorts or flash your cleavage. I don't understand why some people find this so difficult to grasp). See www.morocco-travel.com; e-mail: info@realmorocco.com; or call: 01380 828533. I can't imagine a child who wouldn't be thrilled by Marrakech, where you have culture, beauty, delicious food, extraordinary sights, and can escape into the Atlas mountains or into the desert (on horse- or camel-back) for a (dramatic) change of scenery.

The vast site **www.holiday-rentals.com** has thousands of houses to rent all over the world, from the sublime to the (almost) ridiculous, from the exorbitant to the true bargain. Magazines with private ads worth scouring are the *London Review of Books* and the *Spectator*, along with *The Lady* for Cornwall/Jersey. Also bear in mind house swaps: provided everyone is scrupulously honest about what they have on offer, these can work very well, and some of the houses are amazing. Have a look at the very impressive **www.homelink.org** for a flavour of what's available.

Wedding Dress

t my boarding school in the Home Counties, we were allowed seven objects on top of our chest of drawers. I arrived, aged thirteen, in the middle of the spring term, freshly expelled from my French-speaking London day school and completely unfamiliar, Enid Blyton aside, with English boarding schools and what might go on inside them. I remember being especially startled by these peculiar little drawer-top displays: there'd been no mention of them in *Mallory Towers*. They were the first things I saw after tea on my first day (during which tea the housemistress told me off for wearing the wrong socks – pale blue, which meant games, not 'mufti'. I'd been at the school an hour. When you're thirteen and English isn't yet your first language, you don't say, 'What the fuck's mufti, and why are you legislating about socks?' You just feel cripplingly ignorant and stupid; also foreign. But it's not all bad, because then, in this case, someone smiles at you conspiratorially, rolls their eyes behind the housemistress's back, and you are still friends twenty-five years later. Aah).

But back to the chests of drawers. Almost without exception, the displays consisted of the following, in order of prominence:

1. rosettes won at gymkhanas
2. pictures of mournful-looking horses
3. aerial photographs of 'home'
4. box of Kleenex
5. book
6. lone china trinket
7. hairbrush (comb wedged in).

Odd enough for a girl who is used to spending her time roaming,
not on horseback, about the King's Road and whose house has a
number, not a name. Odder still, my new schoolfriends, it seemed,
weren't so hot on the old pictures of Mummy and Daddy — though
why should they be, really, given that some of them were packed
orf to boarding schools straight after their seventh birthdays?

But I had brought a lot of pictures — of my sisters, of my
grandparents, and of Mummy and Daddy, or rather Mummy
and step-Daddy. I had too many: more than seven. And anyway,
I wanted to fit in, and display my brush and comb like the others,
prominently enough to atone for my lack of rosettes and
ignorance of the meaning of the word 'gymkhana'. Little else
to do, then, than to perform a painful on-the-spot cull: all my
photographs went into a drawer, except for one of my infant
sisters and one, carefully prised years before out of a long-
forgotten photo album of my mother's, of her and my father
on their wedding day.

I don't know what's happened to the
photograph: it floats about, and just when
I think it's lost it suddenly reappears. I used
to carry it around with me everywhere. My
mother, ravishingly beautiful, is smiling
up at my father, who is in army uniform
(I don't know why. He must have been in
the army at some point after military
service, I suppose — it's an odd sort of
thought; improbable). My mother's
enormous eyes are lined with black
eyeliner (it was 1964), and her hair is
piled up in a very shiny, very high
chignon. She is wearing a sari, with gold
embroidery, I think — the photograph
is black and white. I know all children
think their mothers are beautiful, but

mine, even objectively, looks almost excessively gorgeous.
My father looks pleased; he is laughing and holding the eternal
cigarette. My mother has amazing hands, with long fingernails that
look like shells. She is seventeen, he is thirty-five. And there they
are, frozen in time with their flutes of champagne, briefly happy
on my grandmother's lawn.

By the time I went to my boarding school, I had been living
in England for four years, and pretty much thought of my
stepfather as my father. Which he was, in the day-to-day sense:
I saw my actual father only for parts of the holidays. I thought
of my mother, stepfather and sisters as my actual family, and of
my family in Brussels as something more complicated: intensely
real to me when I was with them, but more problematically
nebulous when I wasn't. The exception was my grandmother,
whose biweekly letters (with pressed flowers, always, and tear
stains, sometimes) kept her omnipresent in my head.

The point I am trying to make is that this was a really curious
photograph for me to single out and cherish quite so much,
let alone display so prominently: it didn't represent anything I
actually *knew* (my parents separated when I was two). Neither did
it represent anything I actually hankered after: I had no desire,
then or ever, to see my parents maritally reunited. But there was
my mother on her wedding day, an image so potent and so iconic
that I cared for it passionately – or even dispassionately, on
purely symbolic and aesthetic grounds.

I was older than her when I got married; I was twenty-six. And I
was pregnant, and I'm sure that at the back of my head, somewhere
in among the decisions about the dress and the make-up and the
shoes and the jewellery, was the idea that one day, regardless of
what might happen in the interim, children of mine might want
a photograph of me and their father on our wedding day, smiling
into the camera, looking glamorous and young and full of hope.

I kept thinking about this: about how my wedding dress would,
perhaps, come to symbolize so much for the child I was carrying.

I became obsessed by the idea of the dress, and eventually ended up with the dress of my dreams. And now . . . Well, now I'm separated, and besides, what do you do with your wedding dress once it's served its purpose? Mine sits now, boxed up, in the empty ceiling space above the guest loo. It's a big box: it also accommodates my seventeen-foot train. I really want to look at it, sometimes, and I get as far as setting up the stepladder, but then . . . what? I don't know — I never make it past unfolding the ladder. For all I know, the dress has got the moth, and is now a little pile of dust. And I guess the garland that held my veil — lily of the valley and ranunculus — has disintegrated by now. Or maybe it's still there, miraculously preserved. I can't bring myself to find out.

Wedding dresses are, really, the embodiment of all those transfiguring hopes we have about shopping: for one day, in the right wedding dress, you just are IT. If you don't believe in the redemptive power of shopping, I expect you'd be happy to be married in a potato sack, as long as you had the man you loved by your side. Not me. I wanted all the stops pulled right out, and then out again.

It was *so* beautiful, my wedding dress: it was a couture number, with a corseted bodice, three-quarter sleeves and a full, but not wide, skirt. The corset — so corsety that my bosoms looked exactly like a bottom — was embroidered with tiny flowers, copied from some eighteenth-century fabric. My shoes were white embroidered satin; my figure was a perfect hourglass; my waist — I was three months pregnant, which played havoc with the fittings — appeared tiny. There were layers and layers of butter-soft net (tulle?) under the skirt, which made it impossible to go to the loo without a couple of helpers. I will never forget the fittings — at the designer's studio, at my flat, but especially at his, with the pale spring sunshine coming in through the living-room windows and him faffing about with pins in his mouth, gossiping and laughing and occasionally stopping our chatter by saying something so sweet and nice — 'I quite want to marry you myself' — that the whole

experience became — and I know what a nauseating word this is
to use — magical. Priding myself on realistic expectations, I hadn't
intended to feel 'like a princess' on my wedding day, but I did.

He took everything in hand, the designer, from the seduction
of my stepfather (who was footing the bill) to the bridesmaids'
and pageboys' outfits, to the flowers, to make-up. My sisters,
then aged thirteen and fifteen, turned into eighteenth-century
shepherdesses, the freshest, prettiest creatures you've ever seen,
with mini-corsets and little straw hats, trailing green ribbons and
flowers. I got a make-up artist* to apply his expertise to my face,
and a hairdresser who teased and pulled and hairpieced my hair
into — into an approximation of my mother's wedding-day hair,
funnily enough.

* I still sometimes get make-up artists to 'do' my face if it's a very special
occasion. You could ring an agency and get one to come to your house, but
it would cost a fortune. The best thing to do is to go to various department
stores or specialist make-up shops and get a makeover as often as you can.
 Eventually, you find someone who makes you look amazing — though this is
one of those processes where you have to kiss a lot of frogs and not mind
walking home with an orange face. And then you ask them if they do private
work, and they say yes, and lo! You now have your very own make-up artist.
Mine costs £40 a time — not cheaporama, but worth it twice a year.

It's odd how much hope you can instil in a dress, in a piece of cloth. For me, as for anyone who does the full number when they get married, it was absolutely central to the day — more so than anything, which can't be quite right if you think about it. My husband, waiting at the other end of the interminable aisle, had tears in his eyes as I walked down towards him, my knees literally knocking together under my millions of underskirts, leaning on my father's steadying arm for support. I'd always thought both my father and my stepfather would give me away, but by this time my stepfather — the man who'd effectively brought me up for seventeen years — and mother were hastily divorced, and on absolute non-speakers: he wasn't even at the wedding. (I left from his house, though, that morning: we had a party, and when I got into the car we cried.) And then I tried to be polite and invited the man my mother had remarried to give me away too, assuming that he would say something about being touched etc., but how he couldn't possibly. Far from it: there he was, and there was my dad, and me in the middle, sailing down the aisle like a triple-prowed ship. Later, he made a speech which was all his love for my mother. I remember thinking, But it's *my* day, stop talking about yourselves. My father also made a speech which moved me to tears, not least because I knew that my stepfather (the first one, not the aisle-walker) had helped him write it.

In the evening, after the party and the after-party and the case of champagne summoned up from room service, I went into our hotel bathroom. My brand-new husband was lying on the bed; we were both very giggly. He'd unlaced me; I stepped out of the dress and noticed that my torso was covered in red marks, from where the corset bones had bitten in. I peeled off my false eyelashes and laid them on the side of the sink. I unpinned my hair, took off my hairpiece and laid it by the eyelashes: a gruesome little shrine to artifice. I washed my face, and all the make-up off it, and I was myself again, my wedding day over.

But I'm having to strain to remember all of that. What I remember most about the day is me in my dress. And yes, *of course* my children treasure our wedding pictures, which are scattered all over the house. My eldest son always picks up the same one — my former husband and I are walking back down the aisle, laughing — and says the same thing: 'You look so happy on your wedding day, Mummy.' And we were. It really did its job, that dress.

Since there's always comedy, I'll just add a postscript. My father was very proud of his video camera and had started filming at about 8 on my wedding-day morning, not finishing until late at night. His right eye had been permanently glued to the viewfinder, except when he'd made his speech. Anyway, he went off back to Brussels, saying he'd edit the material down and that our special wedding tape would arrive a couple of weeks later, when we came back from honeymoon.

And, indeed, there it was — 180 minutes: three hours' worth, heavy with promise. I read the note quickly — 'very long . . . hours of tape . . . edited down . . . holiday' — without really taking in much more of what it said. We poured ourselves glasses of wine and settled down on the sofa, almost hopping with anticipation of our evening's viewing. Our lovely wedding day! Preserved for ever! Just as well, we agreed, as it had seemed to pass in such a blur. We pressed Play. There I was, getting ready. Oh, and there we were at the reception, already. There we were dancing. There was my father's voice picked up by the mike, propositioning a dozen or so women as he filmed (' 'Ello.' 'Oh, er, hello'). And then, precisely eight minutes in, there was a tabby cat. In the sunshine. By a caravan. Eh? We fast-forwarded. There were now some red-faced strangers laughing and having lunch up a mountain. Then back to the cat and the caravan. Some Alpine flowers . . . some road . . . the inevitable Kawasaki . . . 'Give me the remote,' said my husband.

As he frantically forwarded and rewound the tape, I re-read the accompanying note. The video of the wedding, my father had written, went on a bit. Very nice and so on, but dull after a while — you know what weddings are like ('Not as well as *you* do,' I muttered to myself). So he'd left the best bits in, but they came to only eight minutes. So, for an extra treat, he had added footage from his last holiday! Just for us! For two hours and fifty-two minutes! A solo holiday, I might add, with only this strange cat and whoever he happened to encounter in restaurants (and filmed at loving length) for company. One of the reasons I really love my ex-husband is that, whenever he reminds me of this, which he did at supper last week, we literally hyperventilate with laughter, just as we did the first time — once we'd got over the shock.

Let's get practical. As I was just saying, all our shopping hopes of metamorphosis come together as one when we set out to buy a wedding dress: the dress will come to symbolize the day, the ceremony, the party, the vows, the marriage itself, for all eternity — no wonder choosing one is such agony. It is particularly difficult if you are old — and let's face it, these days many of us practically Zimmer down the aisle.

I have been vaguely (oh, how coy) thinking about remarriage myself, and wondering what on earth I would wear if I ever did it again: I am, after all, thirty-seven, convex of stomach, and a mother of two. I'm guessing white would be pushing it, but maybe I'm wrong: I've seen forty-year-old brides, some with previous, sail blithely down the aisle in white, like freakily overgrown little girls about to take their first communion. It's a bit of a troubling sight, not least because the middle-aged insistence on the childhood fantasy of 'looking like a princess' on your wedding day is both emotionally poignant (you want to sob) and deeply comical (you want to howl with laughter), to say nothing of aesthetically bizarre in a Havisham kind of a way.

There is, I think, a cut-off point for the meringue, and this must be thirty: any older, and you're dangerously close to *Whatever Happened to Baby Jane?* territory. Actually, I'm being overly diplomatic — I personally believe that meringues are for child-brides only. Still, if you must, then thirty, absolute tops. Looking bride-like is one thing, looking grotesquely muttonish quite another.

There is also a question mark over the whole traditional church-wedding thing if you are older: do you really want to be 'given away' by your daddy if you're forty-three and he's eighty? The pulling back of the veil — 'here is my virgin child; she is yours now' — is surely problematic, especially if people have been cohabiting for the past ten years and have three children. It's odd in other ways, too: you've probably got a good job, pay your own mortgage — you may even be paying for your own wedding. Although I am personally massively in favour of church weddings, I think they need toning down beyond a certain age: no acres of white lace, no veil, no matronly bridesmaids, and instead the loveliest, most column-like dress you can find, white if you must, and lots of children, flowers and jollity. There is also quite a lot to be said for a small church wedding — family and closest friends — followed by a huge party for everyone else. Vows are, after all, very private things: you don't really need anyone else there but you, your beloved, the priest and a couple of witnesses. We adhere too closely to the traditional blueprint for weddings, I think, and it can look very awkward: we must learn to differentiate between the wedding of two twenty-year-olds and of two people old enough to be their parents, and adapt how we look accordingly.

WHAT TO GET MARRIED IN

I can't tell you where to get your wedding dress from, and anyway part of the fun is seeking it out. If you're young, you can wear anything you like. If you're above thirty, think about:

- An ultra-luxe take on bohemian chic: beautiful fabrics; understated but prominent jewellery – beads, chokers, bangles; bits of fur, if it's winter; fluid, flowing lines (nothing tight); vintage. But shop carefully, otherwise you'll end up looking like a bag lady, or Helena Bonham-Carter. My favourite new shop is the L Boutique, 28 Chepstow Corner, Chepstow Place, London W2 4XE; tel: 020 7243 9190; www.thelboutique.com, who will make you something heavenly if any of the above appeal, and kit you out with matching jewels, to say nothing of feathers, corsages and other exquisitely beautiful, opulent accessories. Not just for weddings either, and there's ready-to-wear as well as made-to-measure.

- A very classic, very stylized take on old Audrey Hepburn: no one's ever gone wrong in a fitted cocktail dress and little heels, or in its modern-day equivalent, the fitted white suit. After a shaky period a couple of years ago, these are now a classic, and very sexy if you wear nothing underneath (assuming you're not an H-cup, obviously).

- Any legitimately 'ethnic' (aaargh – though not as bad as my grandmother referring to me as her 'Eurasian' granddaughter) option open to you, with the emphasis on 'legitimately': please, please don't wear a sari if you're not at least partly Asian, for instance. It's not 'flattering to Indians' – it's just crass and it looks stupid. But if you're fortunate enough to have some ancestry to plunder, go for it. If I ever do the marriage thing again, I'm thinking of going full Bollywood (which would be pleasingly comical if my Scottish boyfriend recognized the goodness of kilts, which – alas – he does not). And if I were even remotely Nigerian or Chinese I'd have a field day.

Yet another note of warning: no meringues, but don't, for God's sake, go too far the other way either. Some women, in an attempt to show that they understand the lessons of the age thing, go for an overdone, been-around-the-block rock chick self-consciously 'trendy' look: the non-virginal Gothic whore, for instance. It's the evil twin of the muttonish, this deliberately 'ironic' post-meringue look, and it doesn't work either. You just look old.

Long hair, unless you're young, should go up. There is nothing more grimly muttonish than 'girlish' locks flicking about everywhere and getting into

the pudding. If your hair is curly, it'll frizz with the heat of the party; if your hair is limp, you'll get Flat Head Syndrome within hours. Up it goes, in a taut chignon, possibly embellished by a hairpiece (see page 44).

Everyone is going to be looking at your ring all day: you need to sort out your hands. Have a manicure, obviously, but avoid nail extensions and anything too obviously 'done', like a French manicure (very dated, also common). Short-to-medium nails, buffed or painted a neutral colour, are best, because they work to great effect whether your hands are beautiful or hideous (and hands, as we have seen, show age more quickly than faces). Avoid coloured nail polish: it's very bizarre on brides, and makes you look like you're auditioning for a part in *Nuptial Nymphos*. And do your feet. I went to a party recently where the bride, immaculate and beautiful, had gnarled yellow toenails peeping out of her Choos.

The same goes for make-up: less-is-more is the look you want to go for, even though of course it might involve a veritable truckload of slap. No one wants to look overly reliant on make-up on their wedding day, so no violent lipstick (unless you're going for the bare face, red lips thing, see page 91), no fake tan, not too much shine. This is really one occasion where the amusing eyeshadows in shades of iridescent poisonous green and fluoro canary yellow should stay firmly at home.

And do think about your underthings. When I got married, I was sent off to get proper 'foundation garments' from Rigby and Peller* – any good lingerie shop would do – and they made all the difference. We're not talking wispy little bits of lace, but properly constructed boned things, more orthopaedic than alluring. Of course, it depends on what you're wearing, and on your shape – I expect if one were a size 8 it would be rather sexy to wear a meringue with nothing underneath. But if there are any areas of your bod that you're not 100 per cent delighted with, foundation garments will fix them. There's nothing more boring than spending your wedding day trying to remember to breathe in/not lean forwards too much in case your tits fall out.

---

* You can buy online at www.rigbyandpeller.com, but I wouldn't – they are brilliant at fitting, and the whole point is being measured properly. The actual shops are at 22A Conduit Street, London W1S 2XP; tel: 020 7 491 2200, and 2 Hans Road, London SW3 1RX; tel: 020 7589 9293.

Mothers
and Children

A h, the little darlings. When my sister Amaryllis had just started school and was learning to write, she penned the following:

God who macs the sky
God who makes the art
Evrything above
Are gret
God who macs the clauds
God who macs the fich
God who make the CHOPS
Are grat!

A remarkable little verse, I think we'd all agree: you can just feel all the tremulous excitement of the last line (she was only five at the time), talk about eloquence — if not spelling. This says it all, really, which is why this book is called what it is. My mother didn't drag my little sisters out shopping with her for ages, and then, inevitably, one day she did. The results, as seen in the above poem, were cataclysmic. Children love The Shops, with a passion and an all-devouring hunger that are both terrifying: they want everything. What do you do? We've all seen — we've all had — children that fling themselves about on the floor because you are disinclined to buy them yet another horrible bit of primary-coloured plastic or bag of tooth-rotting sweeties in the shape of aliens. You blush with shame, and go all prickly about the armpits, because there are always people watching, and every single one of them is thinking 'spoilt brat' — a very hypocritical reaction, but a universal one none the less. So your own response becomes ridiculous: you either try and have a rational discussion, in the manner of Isaiah Berlin and Richard Rorty discussing the limits of pragmatism; or you lose your temper in a completely disproportionate way, and end up buying the wretched thing to atone for having just had an epi at a three-year-old child.

I think we do indulge our children to a really ludicrous extent: they more or less have everything they want, whether they're with you at the supermarket, merrily piling the trolley high with Frosties and toxic-looking cakes, or you're at The Shops proper and don't see how buying another Playmobil figure is really going to do very much harm – plus, it's bound to keep them quiet over lunch (plus, well, it's Playmobil, innit. It's *educational*, in a way: not trash. See also Lego). When I worked in an office, as opposed to at home, I was always coming back with some trinket or other – really I might as well have been a Victorian suitor, attaching a note about how the enclosed was a humble token of my esteem. I thought it made me a better parent, to keep giving them this *stuff*, because they'd be bound to see how much I thought about them all day and how much I loved them. They were aged three and six months.

Nevertheless, I carried merrily on in this manner for ages – years – even though I'd stopped going out to work. And then one day I realized, as we all do at some point, that 98 per cent of the toys the children had were never played with, and just sat on shelves, looking mournful. That's the thing about having an embarrassment of choice, especially if you're small: you just stick to Blue Bunny or your train set, and are perfectly happy doing so.

So then I culled: heaps and heaps of toys were dropped off at local schools, nurseries, hospitals and hospices (though not books: I always say yes if I'm asked to buy books, no matter how dire or barely literate, on the basis that anything at all that creates an interest in reading is emphatically A Good Thing). I've been culling ever since, twice a year – though now, of course, the children help me by actively participating in the cull. Howls of protest initially, but not any more: the boys are now old enough to understand, and be (temporarily) appalled by, the fact that some children don't have any toys at all. Culls, by the way, are great: I cull my own wardrobe twice a year, and the house's contents. It's one thing to be acquisitive and another to just sit there like a pig wallowing in excess mud. And after the culls you feel community-spirited and decent, for about three seconds.

I think this is the only reasonable response to the tide of toys that otherwise keeps on coming. Just as my house is always drowning in paper, no matter how hard I try to wade through it every now and then — newspapers, magazines, notes, manuscripts, book proofs, letters, bills, bills, bills — so the children's bedroom becomes awash with toys even weeks after one of the culls: swapped toys, pocket money toys, presents. Which reminds me: it is quite hard to get excited about presents if you're bought everything you ever want.

This is not to suggest that children should be forced to play with twigs and pebbles, give or take the odd peg dolly. But I do think that, if you have the kind of overstocked playroom that is more like a toy shop than part of a family house, you are making a rod to break everyone's back with — your children's as well as your own. It is tempting, of course, if you are time-poor and cash-rich, to express your devotion by the ceaseless purchasing of unnecessary toys — but it doesn't work: it creates brats, *always and without exception*.

Having said all that, the following boxes give some places to get kids' toys from, and some suggestions. Hopefully, their contents are less inane than they might be, and may even encourage imaginative play. We live in hope.

REALLY LOVELY THINGS
TO GIVE CHILDREN

I'm mad about Insect Lore, and so are my children – and their products are among the most successful birthday presents we've ever given. This is because they're ALIVE (NB: This slightly freaks some parents out, and some especially urban children. Never mind – they need to learn). Insect Lore supplies bugs, including butterflies, which come to you as caterpillars. You browse online at www.insectlore.co.uk, or call 01908 563 338, Mon–Fri, 9–5, for a catalogue, and then, having placed your order for, say, the Butterfly Garden (£17), you get a glass full of green gunk (caterpillar food), five live Painted Lady caterpillars, and a big cardboard hatching house with see-through 'windows'. You follow your instructions and get to see the whole process, until, eventually, your actual butterflies hatch – at which point, having observed them and given them names, you set them free in your garden (in which they tend to hang out friendlily for the duration of their brief little lives). You can also order a Hopper Dome – locusts; or giant land snails; or ladybirds. Insect Lore also sells books, toys, science kits and so on, all bug-related. It's really wonderful, Insect Lore.

The Wooden Toy Catalogue is self-describing: it sells old-fashioned wooden toys with modern appeal – including very good puzzles in up to 192 pieces (which is unusual: wooden jigsaws normally come in no more than twenty); wooden train sets; doll's houses; fortresses and wooden baby toys. Browse and buy online at www.woodentoysonline.co.uk, or call 01303 836900, Mon–Fri, 9–5 (longer in the run-up to Christmas) for a catalogue; Worldwide delivery.

Of course, shopping with small children is actually not that much of a nightmare compared to the total horror of shopping with teenagers. I am going on my own behaviour here: my children are still too young (though both can do a passable impression of a stroppy fifteen-year-old. Not as well as me, however). I was an utter nightmare to shop with: I was foul, and I wanted stuff. It's a monstrously unattractive combination, that. It's one thing to be foul and sit in your bedroom in Gothic gloom, and another to be foul round and round and up and down and in and out of Brent Cross shopping centre.

I've been fascinated by department stores since I was small, a fascination that was dramatically amplified after reading Zola's *Au Bonheur des Dames* during one particularly *longueurs*-packed Belgian holiday. The novel is about an eponymous nineteenth-century department store, and contrasts the triumphant emergence of capitalist economy and Parisian bourgeois society with the slow, cruel decline of a dusty draper's shop, whose misfortune it is to be situated opposite the gleaming new monolith. Which is making the novel sound ghastly even to me – thank God I'm not a book critic – but it's not; it's a complete page-turner* about the consumer society, greed, fashion and instant gratification.

Brent Cross shopping centre was a precursor to Bluewater and its ilk: all the debatable goodness of the American shopping mall brought to north London, with dozens and dozens of shops under one roof. There was a John Lewis, with a particularly well-stocked hosiery department – rows and rows of 99p Christian Dior tights in puce, bright yellow, electric blue – a Miss Selfridge (swoon), a huge Marks & Spencer, and it was between these three that my poor mother and I (inevitably mutinous, and wearing too many earrings) lurched. Oh, and there was C&A. Just before I left for boarding school, my mother and stepfather took me to C&A and bought me a polka-dotted yellow dress. It had a fitted bodice,

 * Emile Zola, *Au Bonheur des Dames*, edited by Robin Buss (Penguin, £7.99).

a wide smocked waist and a straightish skirt. This was the dress
I wore with the criminal non-mufti pale blue socks for my first
dinner at my new school. It sticks in my head like glue.

My mother also liked taking me to M&S, which I was prejudiced
against enough to really crank up the eye rolling and desperate
sighing over. Presumably, perfectly reasonably, she wanted to get
whatever I needed in between stocking up on Babygros (she had
two small daughters) and eggs, and didn't see why M&S should
be considered such a hardship by me.

She developed quite a crafty technique, my mum: she'd hold
up some unexciting garment or other and say, 'Oh! How absolutely
amazing! Can it really be . . . Why, yes. This is a *direct* copy of Saint
Laurent! Look, India. Look at the neckline! Look at the red, like
. . . garnets gleaming in the sun.' This worked once or twice, when
some dress she was holding up did indeed, somehow, transform
itself through the miracle of good cutting from drab on the hanger
to fab on the body – though I think it is perhaps overly optimistic to
believe that the designers at M&S, talented as they no doubt were,
scoured the Parisian catwalk for their designs and ripped off the
secrets of aged seamstresses in couture *ateliers*.

Nevertheless, emboldened by her success, my mother took to
employing the Saint Laurent Method on all M&S clothes, from pants
(in the knicker sense) to warm, cosy anoraks ('Pure Givenchy! How
do they do it?'). She also, to my utter and crippling mortification,
insisted that I try things on there and then, on the Marks & Spencer
floor, saying, at the top of her voice, that no one would look, since no
one was remotely interested in my thighs. Writing this, I am actually
trying to remember whether M&S had changing rooms at all: I'm
thinking that perhaps they didn't, and that perhaps this purgatorial
ritual was commonplace, though I don't remember anyone else,
crimson with shame, standing in their pants and tights for those
few seconds before stepping into the proffered pair of trousers,
surrounded by happy shoppers and – always – Hassidim. (I especially
remember the Hassidim because my mother has fairly robust

views on Palestine, which she is not shy about sharing, then or now. Over the years, some of these trips to Brent Cross became occasions to educate me about the Middle East. I'd say, 'Mummy, shush. *We're surrounded by Orthodox Jews,*' and she'd say, 'Good. I absolutely love Jews. It's just the Israelis I can't stand').

If you were wearing a skirt, obviously, you could pull the new skirt on underneath, but for some reason I was always wearing trousers, and trousers ('Dior copies! The brilliance!') were what I needed to try on. You don't see that many fourteen-year-olds in their pants standing scarlet-faced in the middle of M&S any more. I was a pioneer.

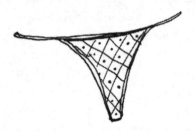

This calvary with the pants and the Hassidim was necessary, because I knew that if I complied in M&S, we'd maybe get to go to Miss Selfridge afterwards. Miss Selfridge was the promised land, with its mannequins in spiky fluorescent wigs, its hangers dripping with tight, low-cut things, not in colours like sun-drenched garnets but in BLACK: skirts that looked like spider's webs, vaguely Goth tops, short skirts, tight T-shirts . . . heaven. Well, heaven for me – only sometimes heaven for my mother. And I do see her problem here: from a relatively early age, one of my sartorial role models has been the prostitute (glamorized ideal of) – not so much now, as I approach forty, but in my prime. This was partly to do with having a raving beauty as a mother* –

* I think this is not uncommon: see also the late Paula Yates, whose boho-slapper wardrobe, while actually managing the rare feat of arguably making the mutton more attractive than the lamb, spoke volumes about what she felt to be, in her autobiography, the crippling physical beauty of her mother.

a raving, impeccably elegant beauty, whose look I knew I could never successfully approximate. My mother is small and I am five foot ten; she has an elegant little bosom, whereas mine is wench-like; she is classically beautiful with amazing bone structure, whereas I am OK; she is skinny-pinny, I am not. And anyway, no teenager wants to look like their mum, no matter how ravingly gorgeous. Besides, I'd spent my childhood sweetly dressed as Little Miss Square; time, surely, for a change. I think my teenage devotion to working-girl chic may also have had to do with my father's porno mags: the only women I knew with busts like mine were in those magazines, looking not entirely wholesome (unless they were reclining on straw, pretending to be farmers) but clearly desirable none the less.

BRAS FOR BIG BOSOMS

Where, oh where, would one be without Bravissimo? This admirable company sells bras in back sizes 30–40, in cup sizes D–JJ–and nearly all of them are (you may faint with surprise) ATTRACTIVE. If you mooch around department stores all sadly, wishing that you too could have a bra in baby blue or hot pink, instead of some medical-looking mega-number in 'flesh', with outsize straps and six sturdy hooks–well, mooch no more. Browse and buy online at www.bravissimo.com, or call 01926 459 859, Mon–Fri, 8.30–8.30; Sat, 9–5, for a mail-order catalogue. Like so many in this book, they bend over backwards to be helpful (but their bosoms stay pointing at the sky).

Less Bounce sell sports bras in back sizes 28–52, in cup sizes A–H. They're not what you'd call foxy, these garments–but who cares, when they mean you can go trampolining without knocking yourself out? Browse and buy online at www.lessbounce.com, or call 0800 036 3840, Mon–Fri, 9–5, for inquiries and catalogue; worldwide delivery. For international inquiries, call: +44 1980 671 305.

But it is to my mother's tremendous credit that she never actually refused to buy me the clothes I liked; or actively stopped me from wearing them out and about. When I dyed my hair white (no mean feat if it's black to start off with), she said it made my eyes greener. When I decided to get myself tattooed as a seventeenth-birthday present to myself, she dissuaded me from choosing anything too gruesome as an image, but not from the tattoo itself. In earlier years, she'd occasionally look quite cross — once, in Laura Ashley of all places, she pretended she wasn't with me — at whatever I'd decided to wear, but she never actually said, 'No way' or 'Take it off.'

And this is part of the miracle of shopping: sometimes, when she and I hadn't exchanged a civil word in days, I'd try something on in Miss Selfridge, my mother waiting impatiently outside, looking thunderous, and as I came out, her whole face would

BUY YOUR NORMAL-BOSOMED GIRLFRIEND A BRA FROM HERE

By 'normal-bosomed', I mean back size 32–38, cup sizes A–DD. You can get lovely bras for normal bosoms from lots of places – what's good about Splendour is its witty, helpful website, especially the advisory section for men ('If you really don't know her [knicker] size and can't check, **DO NOT BUY LARGE**'). It's a good site for men all round, this. If you're buying your bird a present, they'll invoice you by e-mail and she'll get a gift-wrapped box with no price or receipt, but with a prepaid envelope to send it back in if it doesn't fit. Good diamanté thongs, too. Browse and buy online at www.splendour.com, or call 020 8964 7820, Mon–Fri, 8.30–5.30, for inquiries; worldwide delivery.

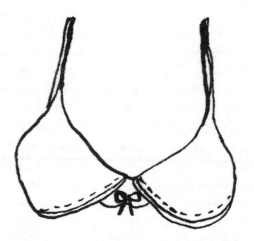

WHAT TO WEAR
IF YOU'RE NOT A SIZE 12

I fall into this category myself, so this advice is from the heart.
1. Don't, whatever you do, buy baggy Fat People's Clothes. THIS IS
CRUCIAL. All designers make these—they are very, very loose, flowing
things, usually waistless, that look amazing if you're a size 10, because
the whole point of them is the contrast between voluminous fabric and
skinny body. Tragically, larger women tend not to understand this and,
delighted that they have finally found things that fit after hours of
traipsing around Selfridges feeling depressed, jubilantly get out their
credit card. The result is disastrous: you end up looking unimaginably
vast, and like you're wearing a gigantic sack. Also, these clothes make
your head look tiny—we're talking diplodocus, really. You want things
with waists, even if you think yours is non-existent, and you definitely
don't want anything that fits loosely on the bosom and then goes all
flowy: I can absolutely guarantee that you'll look heavily pregnant.
What I'm saying is, buy clothes that fit, not clothes that are too loose,
no matter how tempting these seem. You probably have a good bust;
show it off. You're probably curvy; ditto. Don't sausage yourself into a
Spandex tube, but do wear a little cardigan that fits, and a long straight
skirt (beware excess fabric, around the waist or elsewhere—anything
gathered or pleated will make you look like Pregnant Mrs Big Arse).
2. Never, ever wear those heavy, knitted cotton jumpers. There's
something very appealing about these, in a 'Let's pretend it's fall in
Connecticut' way, but they add on a couple of dress sizes and make any
bosoms bigger than a C cup—or maybe even a B—look absolutely
bovine, and any shoulders that aren't narrow look like a shotputter's.
Go for wool, silk or cashmere instead. Bulky tops are a disaster—
if you're worried about being chilly (unlikely: you have plenty of
insulation), carry a shawl around with you.

3. Avoid high necks, particularly with T-shirts, if your bosom is anything other than small. Round-necked T-shirts with a big bust make you look like your breasts start just below your neck and don't really ever end. V-necks, please, as low as you like (within reason). The exception to this is the trusty cashmere cardi — but unbuttoned.

4. What you wear underneath is of the utmost importance. Get a good bra (see page 168) and Pants of Steel for special occasions (see page 58). This can make the most spectacular difference.

5. Bottoms. Mine isn't vast, but I know some that are. In my experience, these are better displayed than covered up. Having a flap of fabric over your big bottom is not flattering; in some instances, it can make people look deformed from the waist down. Show that bottom! Yes, some people might think, 'Blimey, look at her arse — it's huge.' But for every person who does, somebody else will be thinking, 'Fwoar! I am powerfully reminded of J-Lo, and I have the horn.'

6. Stomachs. Grim, innit? Mine is horrendous from two C-sections and no sit-ups. I don't think there's any disguising miracle, stomach-wise — alas. The old Pants of Steel do help, though. I just show my breasts quite a lot and hope that no one's eye travels downwards too much. Try also praying to St Jude, the patron saint of lost causes.

7. Where to shop . . . Anything from Ghost (see page 76), especially long bias-cut skirts. Wrap dresses from Diane von Furstenberg (very flattering, sexy — stockists from www.dvf.com; try also www.net-a-porter.com). Maharishi 'pants' (also net-a-porter). Boden for pottering about in (see page 104). Designers at Debenhams — you occasionally stumble upon a marvel. Topshop's Tall Girl range if you're, er, tall — marvellous long denim skirts with stretch.

soften and she'd say, 'That really suits you' or 'Oh, how lovely' or 'And you could wear the new strappy sandals with it.' She is not what you'd call a conciliatory type, my mother: she wasn't trying to be sweet to make up for some earlier argument. She was genuinely pleased that I looked nice in whatever it was I'd tried on, and was genuinely saying so. And there would be a cessation of hostilities for, ooh, hours sometimes.

So actually, after I'd got over the slouching around looking grumpy and the rolling of eyes, I came to the conclusion that shopping wasn't half useful when it came to what we'd now call bonding. Even in Sainsbury's: too horrid and teenage to say, 'Sorry, and can we be friends now?' I'd pick up some new thing and show it to her, and our common greed would allow us to speak normally to each other while discussing the virtues of, say, undyed haddock. To this day, my mother and I are at utter peace with one another when shopping, whether we're scrutinizing a *pâtisserie* display, trying to choose a cake for tea, or buying shoes together. I am puzzled by those very expensive Tesco ads that showed Jane Horrocks as the daughter and Prunella Scales as the mother, bickering and exasperating each other round the supermarket. In my experience, when push comes to shove, women shopping together — any kind of shopping, any kind of women — always leads to some kind of ceasefire.

Presents
(for R.G.)

I don't believe that there is anyone on earth, young or old, rich or poor, who doesn't love presents. You may not be as extreme as the late Barbara Skelton, whose sometime diary entry – 'My birthday. Insufficient fuss made' – rings so achingly true for more than a few of us, but that doesn't mean that the unnatural view of presents-as-ordeals is gaining ground. In my experience, people who say, 'No, I honestly don't want anything for my birthday,' are a) falsely modest, b) nauseatingly holier-than-thou (in which case you say, 'What, not even a donation to your favourite charity?') and c) letting you know, in the coarsest manner imaginable, that they certainly won't be remembering *your* birthday. Or – minute likelihood, but I suppose possible – so rich that there is genuinely nothing that they want. Even so, though, it's awful to be so rich that you are jaded. Even the grotesquely rich should be able to appreciate a little bunch of perfect violets, or some chocolate-dipped apricots (from Prestat, page 62), and if they can't, they're too rich and should give some of their money away.

CHARITIES

Yes, I know – too little, too late. You can't write a whole book about the joys of shopping and then, consumed with guilt, atone for it by bunging in a little box on charities. But it's my book and so I'm going to. Besides I'm not remotely consumed with guilt. I don't see why liking nice cushions should preclude charitable donations. There was a survey recently that showed that comfortably off people simply don't give to charity: the vast majority of charities' income is derived from donations by the super-rich, and from people who don't really have two pennies to rub together. I think this is crap. You know who you are, and you know which charities exist. Numbers are in the *Yellow Pages*; or use the web – it is now very easy to make donations online.

Who on earth would genuinely want to wake up on their birthday morning bloomless, cardless, presentless? You'd slash your wrists, surely. And yet people don't really understand this most fundamental human truth, and ignore or 'forget' people's birthdays, because they're too lazy to buy a bunch of daffs and stick a stamp on a card. We all want to be loved, and if we can't be loved, with some fanfare, on our birthdays, then really what hope is there? And don't be fobbed off with the old 'But you're so special to me that it's your birthday every day, my love' trick. Bollocks to that. It's not your birthday every day — it's your birthday once a year, and trumpets need to sound, metaphorically at least.

If they don't, 'Insufficient fuss made' is about the measure of it: one's disappointment needs to be made public and culprits educated. Sometimes, it really isn't their fault. If you were brought up in a house where, on a good year, your birthday present was a box of chocolates, then obviously you may be likely to think that This Will Do. (If you fall into this category, let me ask you — did it feel good to receive one lone box of Black Magic on your thirteenth birthday? No, it did not. So don't do it to anybody else. Don't pass on the misery on the 'if it was good enough for me' basis. This is what some people still say when they argue for the return of corporal punishment: 'I was beaten and humiliated twice a week at school, and it never did me any harm.'

Sorry, but it's not good enough. Can you imagine expanding
the argument? 'I was stabbed repeatedly in the head, but I'm
still here, so obviously it can't have done me any real harm.
The whingers should buck up.')

This is not, in any sense, meant to imply that sufficient fuss
equals diamond necklaces. The whole point of, and brilliance of,
thoughtful presents is that you absolutely don't need to spend a
fortune. I am deeply suspicious of very expensive presents anyway,
because I think they are often thoughtless: someone's just phoned
Tiffany's and given them a top-limit figure and a credit card
number. Some people may not care, as long as they get the rocks,
but I do. I think it's sad and awful. Having said that, obviously not
all monumentally expensive presents stem from this lame attitude,
and some, of course, are worth dancing a jig of joy for. You can
tell which fall into which category by the giver.

How, then, to educate someone who's rubbish at presents?
Gently. There's no point in having a tantrum and roaring
'INSUFFICIENT FUSS, INSUFFICIENT FUSS' as you
roll round and round the floor, red-faced and choking on your
own sobs. You need to show them, by finding out when their own
birthday is and doing them small birthday kindnesses, followed by
a really fantastic, as in well thought out, present, and handful of
smaller, sillier ones. The very basic kindnesses might include:

- the inevitable breakfast in bed — not just toast and jam but
  delicious pastries, or eggs Benedict, and fresh juice, with really
  good tea or coffee, followed by
- running them a delicious bath, during which you sit and chat to
  them, and bring more tea (I'm assuming a degree of intimacy:
  this wouldn't work for your boss's fiftieth)
- bringing them down to a kitchen table laden with presents,
  flowers, cards and so on
- driving them to work if they usually take the bus, or getting
  them a taxi (or, if it's a weekend, taking them back to bed with

papers — to be read during the digestion process, and followed
by particularly rampant sex)
· meeting them for lunch, or sending a bloom to their desk —
  NOT the old red roses (unless they're almost black Baccarat),
  but something that you've chosen yourself, with care; if you're
  a man, choose masses of the same thing in the same colour
  and you won't go very wrong

— and so on, throughout the day, but not so madly or extravagantly
that they feel uncomfortable, or indeed stalked. The kindnesses
work for all ages: I used to paint enormous posters on brown
paper for my little sisters and pin them all over the house, so
that from the moment they woke up they'd see signs saying, for
instance, 'How fine, how very fine/To wake up and be NINE'.
When my mother was broke and I was small, she'd decorate one
of the kitchen chairs with garlands of Christmas tree and glitter
(I was born in December), and make me a 'throne' to eat my
breakfast porridge at. When you're five, believe me, this is just
unimaginably wonderful. A friend of mine, who wanted to do
something spectacular for his child but had no money for a grand
present (doubly sad as he only sees the son every other weekend),
recently made an entire huge 'boat' out of cardboard boxes people
had thrown out by their bins (it took him ages to collect them all),
and invited his son to come on a sea trip in it with him. They
packed sandwiches for lunch, ducked from the bigger waves,
took turns steering, said hello to imaginary sea creatures, and
my friend kept his ecstatic four-year-old entertained with stories
and songs about the sea for hours on end. I know it sounds a bit
cutesy to tell people to make celebration posters or ships out of
cardboard, but the point is that such creations just delight people,
and make them happy, and are the very essence of good presents.
If you start doing this with your children, they'll do it for their
children and anyone else they love, and everybody will have happy
birthdays. I don't want to sound like Pollyanna, skippety-skipping

along, spreading the goodness, and I am aware that that is precisely what I do sound like. I don't care. Birthdays are totally great — and they should be. All presents are totally great. Now, here are some ideas.

Birth
- A stripy cashmere blanket from www.brora.co.uk; for inquiries, call: 020 7736 9944. Beautiful, soft, warm, and if you get a reasonable size, it can be their comforter for years to come.

Christening
- Start laying down wine for them via Berry Bros (see page 39). People think only very grand or rich godparents do this, but that's wrong. Even if you lay down only one fantastic bottle a year, they'll have eighteen wonderful things to drink when they come of age – and how nice, for instance, to drink a bottle that was laid down at your christening on the night you get engaged. If you lay down one fantastic *case* – again, it needn't be Margaux – then your godchild will have the beginnings of their own proper cellar.
- I am also a great believer in charm bracelets, starting from birth or christening, but I know some people don't like them. Everybody likes wine, though.

Boys and Girls Aged Four
- Swimming lessons. The school ones aren't enough, and a depressing and unnecessary number of children still die by drowning in Britain each year.

Little Girls of Six–Eight
- A Butterfly Garden from Insect Lore (see page 162).
- All your old lipsticks, pushed into an empty artist's large watercolour box and smoothed into irresistible pinky-red rounds.
- I saw the most amazing girl's dressing-up trunk at Au Nain Bleu in Paris; unfortunately, it was monstrously – really monstrously – expensive. But I don't see why one shouldn't re-create it at home. It was a proper, beautiful trunk. You opened it and there, resting on a false bottom, was a jaw-droppingly exquisite party dress, looking like the wedding dress in a fairy tale. The inside of the trunk lid had pairs of delicate, glittering shoes, handbags, an ornate and magical-looking belt, hair combs and armfuls and armfuls of

jewels. Underneath the trunk's false bottom, the space was crammed with box after box of make-up, from lipsticks to eyeshadows, and more rings, brooches, crowns and jewels than it was possible to count in twenty minutes of staring open-mouthed at the thing. If you're the kind of person who keeps old make-up and old jewellery, and can stretch to buying one lovely dress and a load of glittery plastic shoes, as well as a trunk, you'd make someone very, very happy by emulating this trunk's contents.

Little Boys of Six–Eight

- Giant snails from Insect Lore.
- Hopper Drome from Insect Lore (both page 162).
- A dinosaur egg! Yes, really – a real one. A really, really real one: I've had endless conversations with the nice people at *National Geographic* to make sure dinosaur eggs really still exist. And they do. They're fossilized, obviously. How cool is that? How amazing? They're 65 to 45 million years old, and because they've been dug up reasonably often since about 1995, they're quite easily found on the market, starting at a couple of hundred quid. They won't be around for ever, though. I wouldn't buy them online, although you can, because reputable Fortnum and Mason, of all places, usually have small numbers of them in stock in their Ancient Art department: 181 Piccadilly, London W1A 1ER; 020 7734 8040. To see what dinosaur eggs look like, try Verhult's Fossils online at www.fossil.cjb.net. The most brilliant shop for all fossil/bone-related purchases is Evolution, 120 Spring Street, New York, NY 10012; tel: +1 212 343 1114. Everything they sell is beautiful and extraordinary. Browse online at www.evolutionnyc.com, then phone your order through and they'll ship it to you. Fossils, skeletons, trilobytes, spiders' webs under glass, bones, shells, skulls – amazing.

Slightly Older Boy

- Tuck box from Meg Rivers (see page 48).
- George MacDonald Fraser's books – it is your godmotherly duty to stop your godchild reading crap.
- Practical jokes from www.sillyjokes.com.
- Really good pencils – say Caran d'Ache – and drawing paper.
- A pack of playing cards and *The Penguin Encyclopedia of Card Games* by David Parlett. Cards are such fun, and hardly anyone knows how to play any more, which I think is tragic. A) You're never bored if you can play card games and b) poker and rummy – or Old Maid or Hearts, for novices – are some of the few things you can play *en famille* and actually love every minute of. Very good for getting the generations together, and a necessary social skill, I think. Everyone should know how to play rummy, at the very least.
- A backgammon set – from any toyshop, or if you want to make it the kind of backgammon set they'll keep for ever, one from Pickett (see page 104). Everything I've said about cards applies to backgammon. Also, you can play for money, eventually. Some of us more or less put ourselves through university by playing backgammon.
- Snatch. It's a word game – a variant on that game you can play with Scrabble tiles. Utterly brilliant, utterly addictive, and, since it's not a kids' game *per se*, they'll play it until they're old and decrepit. Get it directly from www.portobellogames.com.

Slightly Older Girl

- A goody box from Lush, www.lush.co.uk, featuring bath bombs, soaps that smell of marzipan, natural skin products that won't give them acne, chocolate massage bars, frozen cubes of shampoo, and more delicious-smelling, deliciously girly things than she'll have ever seen.
- Pencils and paper, as above – maybe also glittery or scented pens.
- Playing cards, backgammon, Snatch (see above).

Teenage Girl

- She's probably going through that 'experimental' phase, and not liking her hair. Before she chops it all off and dyes it mahogany, book her an imaging consultancy atTrendco (see page 44), so she can try out different styles and colours without doing damage to her actual own hair.
- Cheap CDs. They're all £9.99, including the chart stuff, from CDWow! at www.cd-wow.com, although you might like to broaden her musical horizons a little at this time and go for classical – don't let her be the kind of adult who doesn't know Mozart from Wagner. Ditto DVDs: send her proper films – *L'Atalante*, *Les Enfants du Paradis*, *The Song of Bernadette* and other classics.
- Her first facial (see page 82). No, it's not too early, and she'll thank you for it when she's old enough to be a remarkably well-preserved godmother herself.
- Scent. A woman needs a signature scent, and teenage girls are depressed enough without needing to walk around smelling of horrible plasticky mass-produced fragrance. Send her to Les Senteurs (see page 86) to chose her own scent, or get them to send her some samples to choose from; once she's found it, replenish her supplies by mail order.
- An eyebrow lesson. I don't know why plucking should be such an essential teenage pastime, but it is – and your eyebrows end up ruined. Take her to get her brows down properly by any of the people on pages 20–21.
- A copy of *Forever Amber* (see page 108).

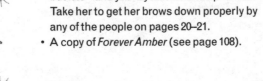

Teenage Boy
- CDs from CDWow! and films (as above).
- A visit to a facialist (see page 82) to stave off grotty, confidence-trashing teenage skin.
- Beautiful and effective shaving equipment from D. R. Harris (see page 42): badger brushes and almond soap.
- Delicious aftershave from Les Senteurs (see page 86) – save your godson from smelling like an elderly gigolo.
- A karaoke machine, delivered in a plain brown wrapper, from EM Karaoke (see page 135) – all teenage boys like pretending they're rock stars. Girls too, come to think of it. And their mums and dads. An excellent present all round, then.

University
- A Starving Student Box from Meg Rivers (see page 48) at the beginning of each term (or wait a bit, until they've run out of money and are living on spaghetti with mousetrap).
- The best literary novel of the moment at the start of each holiday.
- A mini-cooler (see page 115) to have in their room – saves flatmates nicking their beer.
- A lovely blanket from Melin Tregwynt (see page 112), or a throw from the selection on page 136, because student houses are always cold.
- Something lovely from Antoine & Lilli (404 King's Road, London SW10 0LJ; tel: 202 7349 0033) to brighten up their room.
- Money. I am usually against gifts of money, but in this case they make up in usefulness what they lack in imagination.

Twenty-first Birthday
- Send them a hangover cure (see page 42), to arrive on their birthday morning.
- Their wine will be ready by now, so send them on a wine course before they gulp it all down. Berry Bros (see page 39) does an excellent one.
- Everyman editions of the classics.
- Facials, make-up applications and hairdressing all very welcome the day before the twenty-first party (see page 82).

Moving into Their First Home
- A Roberts radio (from www.qed.com or www.johnlewis.com, see page 122) tuned to Radio 4.
- A huge supermarket shop from any of the online suppliers on page 34, packed with staples – sea salt, brown sugar, pasta, basmati rice, tea, coffee, loo paper, Frosties, timed to arrive on their first day in.
- Cushions and bedding from Puppy (see page 111).
- Scented candle from any of the suppliers on page 135.

Moving in with Boyfriend

- Lovely underwear from Agent Provocateur (www.agentprovocateur.com, also 6 Broadwick Street, London W1F 8HW; tel: 020 7439 0229) or Splendour (see page 169).
- Scent from Frédéric Malle (see page 86).
- *How to Eat* by Nigella Lawson (Chatto & Windus, £17.50).

Moving in with Girlfriend
- Leaping Salmon food kit, to impress on first night (see page 40).
- *How to Eat* (as above).
- Brand-spanking-new underwear from Turnbull and Asser (see page 29).

Engagement Presents
- Beautiful kitchen pans from Divertimenti (see page 122).
- Goose-down bedding (see page 114).

Post-Stag Night
- Voucher for Hair of the Dog treatment from the Refinery (see page 42).

Post-Hen Night
- Voucher to Bliss Spa, or any on page 45.

Buying Their First Home
- On the day they move in, send them a food box from Paxton & Whitfield (see page 37). Better than pizza, and they can enjoy it with one of their bottles of wine.
- A tree or plants from Architectural Plants, Crocus or Keepers Nursery (see pages 50 and 140).

First Baby
- Huge practical online supermarket shop to be delivered to them.
- Ugg boots and attractive pyjamas (see page 107). They're not going to feel like getting properly dressed, but can't receive visitors in stained nightdresses either.
- Pull-ons from Boden (see page 104), for same reason.
- Massages at home from Heaven @ home or Urban Zest (www.urbanzest.co.uk, also 66 Radipole Road, London SW6 5DL; tel: 020 7736 9111).

The best present I've had in recent years was from my youngest
sister: for our birthdays, she made my other sister, my mother,
my stepfather and me a photo album. She'd gone through the
boxes and boxes of old family photographs her parents had lying
around, selected the really significant, lovely ones from the past
twenty-odd years and had them copied. What was especially nice
was that, as is the case with all fragmented families, no one, post-
divorce, had thought to collect all the pictures of happier times:
these had all been tucked away somewhere, as if they were shameful
or no longer relevant. But of course they *were*: they were our
childhoods, regardless of what happened subsequently, and
I practically wanted to cry (in a good way) as I turned the pages.
There were births, marriages, holidays, from toddlerhood to
now. This is an incredibly nice thing to do for anyone – a similar
album would make a wonderful wedding or twenty-first present.
When our beloved au pair's work permit eventually ran out, she
did a variant of the same thing: she presented us with all the best,
funniest pictures from her four years with us, bound in a fat pink
book. Everyone is very fond of photographs, and always taking
them, but actually sitting down to arrange them is not a thing that
most of us manage, despite wishing we could find the time to do
so. I think these completed, ready-to-browse photo albums make
fantastic presents for any significant occasion – they really are the
kind of thing money can't buy.

So the best presents are those that are emotionally resonant in
some way. The second-best presents are those that the givee would
never buy for themselves. I have a table crammed with small, cheap,
glittery photo frames in all sizes: they're the kind of thing I like
when I see, but never actually get round to picking up and buying,
even though they cost under a fiver. Luckily, I have a friend who
does buy them, and the resulting little table display which has come
into existence over three or four years is one of the things I am
really happy to see as I go around doing the dusting – I don't *need*
glittery photo frames, but they make my life more cheerful. We

tend not to buy things like glittery frames, or artificial flowers, or cheap earrings (from Accessorize and Mikey – oh, the bliss) or feather corsages for ourselves. Speaking of the latter . . .

V. V. ROULEAUX

This is an absolutely lovely and evocative shop, especially if you're creative or handy with a needle. It basically sells trimmings and haberdashery: more kinds of ribbon than you knew existed, also tassels, feathers, tie-backs, silk flowers (and leather ones). You can browse the stock online at www.vvrouleaux.com, or call them with your order or for information on 020 7224 5179, Mon–Sat, 9.30–6. This is the number at the flagship store at 6 Marylebone High Street, London W1U 4NJ. They also do an excellent sampling service for £10, whereby you send them a scrap of some fabric which you want to match or embellish and they send you matching samples of trimmings to choose from. This is the place to come to if you want to cheer up an old dress with a flower corsage, or indeed cheer up an old cardigan by giving it a new trim. If you can actually sew, I would imagine V. V. Rouleaux would be your idea of paradise: with stock this beautiful and a tiny bit of imagination, you could create miracles.

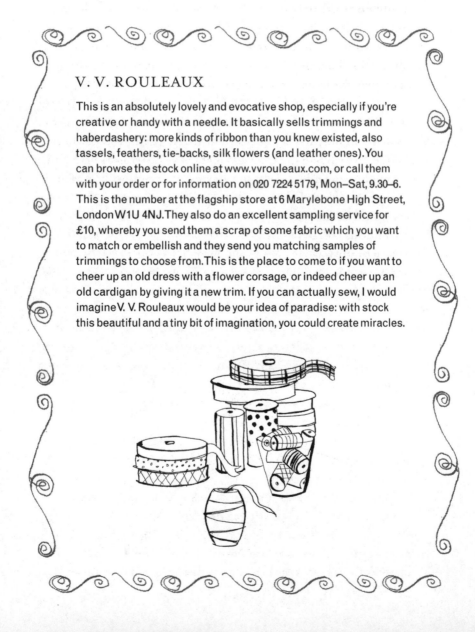

I also don't think that being hard up should necessarily come in the way of present giving — though obviously, if you are absolutely destitute, you're hardly going to have present giving as your number one priority. If you encounter an emergency, though — a relative's birthday that it would be politically disastrous to ignore; your best friend's fortieth — there are a number of things you can do. Anyone with a steady hand can carry out a basic manicure, for instance — and everyone likes being on the receiving end of one, particularly old ladies. I spent years giving my great-aunts manicures, and when my maternal grandmother was dying in hospital last year, my sister Amaryllis did her hands and feet, which had the most dramatically cheering effect. There is something wonderful about unexpected presents, of which this is a slightly melodramatic example: no one imagines a dying old lady would be much fussed about her nails, but sometimes the superfluous is exactly what's needed, and what's most welcome Having pretty nails is a great deal more cheering than having a load of people huddled around your bed sobbing and ululating.

A harassed mother of three may not 'need' a home-made voucher saying she's entitled to an hour-long back rub from you — but, my goodness, she'll love it. And the mother of a new-born who's not sleeping through the night would love the offer of a whole day's baby-sitting far more, if she's anything like me, than boxes of chocolates, potted orchids and expensive baby clothes. A friend in hospital may appreciate the services of a mobile hairdresser more than she'd appreciate an expensive bunch of flowers (they cost the same) — and so on and so on. The best presents are those that show the giver's ingenuity and thoughtfulness — and the worst those that show his or her laziness and lack of imagination.

I love vouchers. We were visiting my sister in Los Angeles years ago and there, on her coffee table, was an incredibly charming book of vouchers she'd made for her then boyfriend, and stapled together. It helps that she can draw – each voucher was like a mini work of art, but actually the intrinsic sweetness of the voucher system wouldn't be irreparably damaged by having typed vouchers on photocopying paper (you can buy them ready-made in some places. Don't. They're called 'Sex Cheques' and seem to be made for people who fear and loathe Bedroom Unpleasantness). My sister's vouchers were specific to her relationship, but depending on who the vouchers were for, you could have some or any of the following:

For Girlfriends
- This voucher is good for one massage/manicure/pedicure, administered by me.
- This voucher is valid for one night's unpaid baby-sitting, or an afternoon, if you prefer, so that you can sleep.
- This voucher entitles you to help yourself to my wardrobe without asking.
- This voucher guarantees that I will tell the truth when you ask me about your new boyfriend, instead of pretending to be surprised when he turns out to be a complete disaster.
- This voucher is good for one girlie weepie, followed by dinner.

For Partners
- This voucher is good for me ungrumpily cooking dinner, to be had on laps, for you and ten of your mates the next time there's a game on that you want to watch.
- This voucher entitles you for one night only to one lot of unreasonably vigorous sexual demands even though I'm so tired that I could teach a junior doctor a thing or two about exhaustion.
- This voucher entitles you to a lobster supper. I will kill the lobster myself and not become hysterical.
- This voucher guarantees one lie-in. I will take the children out early in the morning and let you sleep as long as you like.
- This voucher allows you the right to pull out of a family occasion of your choosing at short notice, without me saying, 'My mother? Ha! What about *your* mother?'

For Children

- This voucher allows you one unlimited night's PlayStation activity without me bursting in and telling you that when I was your age we read Dickens and made our own fun, and my God, MY GOD, what did I do to deserve a houseful of idiot children who sit there staring at the screen and practically dribbling?
- This voucher allows you to have three friends sleeping over without me delivering my teatime lecture on the miracle of vegetable life, complete with lengthy digression on photosynthesis. I will not speak of the utter coolness of veg. You can have pizza.
- This voucher is good for one session of playing football indoors.
- This voucher entitles you to not have to be nice to the guests' strange children for one weekend only.

Curiously, I find that vouchers go down particularly well with children, even otherwise jaded children, who are really delighted to receive them and act upon them at once. Don't be tempted to cheat, though, and prefix any statement with 'if you tidy your room' or 'if you have a good report'. The whole point of the vouchers is that they are *presents* and that there's very little in it for you — apart from a warm loving feeling, natch.

WHERE TO GO IF YOU NEED A PRESENT AND DON'T FANCY SPENDING THE DAY LOOKING

My absolutely number one choice would be Pickett (see page 104), for wonderful leather goods – wallets, notebooks, boxes, bags, albums – in wonderful rich jewelled colours, but also for the most handsome bridge and backgammon sets. For women, there are piles and piles of lovely embroidered, beaded and trimmed pashminas, scarves and shawls, as well as semi-precious jewellery in great luxurious strings, handbags by The Jacksons . . . I could go on and on. It's a treasure trove, and nothing they sell is ugly. As I've said before, this is practically my favourite shop in London.

PRESENTS FOR DADS

Obviously you could roam the streets/net for days and days –
these are ideas for if you're in a hurry:

- Pickett (as above).
- D. R. Harris (see page 42) for old-fashioned brilliantine, lovely fragrant shaving soaps, bone-handled toothbrushes, Pick-Me-Up.
- Anything, pretty much, from the office/personal care sections of the Manufactum catalogue (see page 136), including their very handsome, very useful old-fashioned Rolodex.
- A weathervane from Otter Wrought Iron Products (see page 49).

PRESENTS FOR MUMS

- Pickett (as above).
- Perfume from Les Senteurs (see page 86) or Frédéric Malle mail order (see page 86).
- Anything from David Champion (see page 136).
- A spa treatment or two from the places on page 45.
- Books from Persephone, particularly *Miss Pettigrew Lives for a Day* (see page 108).

ULTIMATE PRESENT FOR PARENTS' IMPRESSIVE WEDDING ANNIVERSARY

A pub for their garden. You'll have to get together with your siblings, and maybe take out a bank loan – but if your parents have managed twenty-five years together, they're worth it (I imagine. I wouldn't know). See Keenmac Pubs (page 142).

But really, nearly all of the things mentioned in the boxes would make marvellous presents, so check the Index. Oh dear, how sad, I've nearly finished. I wish I could write this book in ten volumes.

How to shop

· Buy online. I find my life has changed since I've been shopping
this way: I now have heaps of time on my hands for proper,
recreational shopping at the Actual, rather than virtual, Shops.
Buying all the heavy/bulky/boring/complicated stuff online, or
via mail order, frees you up to spend the odd afternoon having
a lovely time wondering about – maybe buying things, maybe
not – safe from the horrible feeling that you simply HAVE
to get the dinner/a birthday present/school socks in the next
hour, otherwise your world will collapse. Having your weekly
supermarket shop delivered to your door really does do
wonders for your quality of life.

· Don't be intimidated or fobbed off. Very poor service is a staple
of British life, but it doesn't mean you have to put up with it.
Speak out: if a sales assistant is making you feel pressurized and
'forcing' you to make an expensive purchase that you know isn't
quite right, smile and say, 'I don't like feeling pressurized. I'll
look for you if I need help.' If service is entirely absent rather
than tiresomely in-your-face (and our shops do seem to favour
both these extremes, rather than any middle ground), say,
'I need some help/advice, and if you can't help me, I'll go
elsewhere.' Very, very few shops sell things exclusively: if shop
A is rude, unhelpful or uninterested, try shops B, C and D,
and tell your mates when you've found somewhere friendly –
spread the good news. Friendly shops deserve to be patronized;
unfriendly shops deserve to go bust. And don't ever feel that
the shop is too 'smart' or 'posh' for you. You can shop in your
nightie with a coat on top, if you so wish. Shops that make you
feel small aren't worth patronizing. It's supposed to be a
pleasure, not an ordeal.

· Don't assume that something is good or superior just because it is expensive. Anyone who's ever worked in a shop will tell you about astronomical mark-ups. Mark-ups are, obviously, a necessity if you're running a business, but some people try it on and crank up the percentage simply because they can get away with it. If something seems shoddy to you, despite the hefty price tag that's there to tell you it's Quality, trust your instinct.

· Don't assume things are worse because they're cheap. Sometimes they are — it's fairly obvious — and sometimes they aren't. There is no shame in buying cheap things, and a considerable art in mixing them with more expensive ones. Anyone who's, say, an IKEA snob has issues with their own self-esteem, because it is extremely sad, and rather 1980s, to define yourself by what you're sitting on. Anyone who does this, and sneers at you for not doing the same, is a prick. You can safely ignore everything they say.

· There is no such thing as good taste. There is only the taste that's good for you. Don't let anybody tell you otherwise. You want a circular bar with goldfish swimming about inside? You want a circular white plastic bed upholstered in salmon sateen? Go right ahead. The object of the exercise is not to impress the editor of *World of Interiors*. It is to make you happy every time you pour yourself a drink/go for a nap.

- Don't be overambitious: you're not going to be able to get
  Christmas presents for your whole family in one afternoon
  (though with some forward planning, and by using the boxes,
  you might very well get the bulk of it done without leaving
  home). Give yourself time – it's the greatest luxury of all.

- In my experience, it's the little things that really make you happy:
  the armful of cheap glass bangles, the glittery body lotion, the
  stripy mug, the honey jar with a particularly jaunty bee on top.
  These purchases are just as satisfying as spending a fortune on
  a sofa. More, in fact, because they're guilt-free. This is what
  people fail to understand about shopping: some of them feel
  guilty because they don't 'need' the bangles. But if we're talking
  £3.50 for a month's worth of good mood – the same price as a
  decent glass of wine – who's to say that's bad or self-indulgent?

- Set yourself a budget and stick to it, regardless of how flush
  you're feeling. Having a limit means you are forced to be
  ingenious, which is more interesting for you and will result
  in a better purchase, especially if you're buying presents.

- Similarly, do resist the urge to splurge in the belief that this will
  magically make your present better – and, by extension, will
  make you a better and more generous person. Thoughtfulness
  is what makes good presents, not chucking money about.

- Do get organized. Planning shopping outings with military
  precision saves you from that terrible feeling you get when
  you've thought 'I'll just go to the West End and have a look
  around', and find yourself, four hours later, feeling
  claustrophobic in a packed department store. Identify what you
  need, think properly about where you might find it, and stake
  your claim. Unless you actively enjoy it, roaming pointlessly in
  the centre of town can be quite spectacularly unrewarding.

· Shun the big shops. As a rule of thumb, staff are less helpful, the choice is too great, the experience of shopping is too rushed and frenetic. Small local shops and boutiques often have excellent stock, intelligently edited down, and they're friendly and helpful to boot.

· Enjoy yourself. It's the best fun, and it *matters*. It goes without saying that shopping can be political: obviously, if every single one of us stopped buying insecticide-drenched vegetables or battery chickens, they would stop existing. It also matters that something as apparently insignificant as buying a strawberry-flavoured lollipop reminds you of your grandfather, and in some small way comforts you. That's the beauty of shopping: it *always* matters, as I hope this book has shown.

'Our Lady of Pleasure'

(a short story)

.

Funny how friendship can blossom like a rose when you're fourteen — sweet and sudden, just like that, when you're still wearing two pairs of knickers for Gym. Delphine Lacoste came from Normandy to St Bernadette's at the start of the spring term — her hair short, her clothes strange, her temperament instantly built for love. Apart from a pencil case filled with tiny brushes and combs, Delphine brought to the English class nothing but a talent for pranks and a knowledge of adventures, old and modern. She had lots to say about boys and shoes: the only topics then, the only topics now.

The great surprise — surprise, at least, to girls from Norfolk, whose notion of literature was never to let it tangle with the rush for school dinners — was that Delphine carried around in her purse cuttings about writers and books. I remember the purse and its tiny white beads, and how delicate it was in her hand. Well, inside it she kept these yellow cuttings — things from newspapers, lines from poems, and sometimes, beside them, their tidy translations in her curlicued hand. Apart from the memory of Delphine herself, and, of course, the customary hatred of games, I don't suppose I carried much away from my schooldays at St Bernadette's. And yet even now, when I think of those times, I realize that everything I would later enjoy knowing (as opposed to just knowing) came out of that beautiful, beaded purse.

A line from Flaubert — I think — about the relationship between stupidity and martyrdom: Delphine talked about that, about

Charles Bovary, and about the wicked man who sold Emma stuff she didn't need. I just listened, and out of the purse would come another piece of hard-to-understand news from the French world of passion and *things*. I tell you all this only so that you'll understand my fascination with the article that follows. It brings back everything of my schooldays, and all of Delphine is present in the thin paper.

Delphine came in the spring and left in the autumn – that was the way of things then, at that place – but I still remember us lying on our stomachs at the back of the playing fields, reading all those pretty things that were folded away, like tiny possibilities, in Delphine's purse, and the light – my God, there is always light when it comes to such memories, I know, but Delphine's little stories really did shimmer, they did. The point is that the whole matter of Delphine – the whole GO of her, as my Irish husband would say – came back in a flash with this morning's paper. Good God, the whole go of her – here, now, Delphine Lacoste. There was never a one to match her, my lost friend, and now I have a story for my own purse.

I'll just write it out for you. I could spend the day – every day for God's sake, every afternoon if I had them to myself – just remembering this and that. But no, I'll just write it out. You can have it for yourself. Here, straight from page 19 of the *Daily Telegraph*, 14 December 2003, an otherwise quiet day for news.

French Nun
Gets Superior
Welcome Home

In a case that has gripped France for the last fortnight — and has even sparked rumours of interest from Hollywood — a 32-year-old nun from Normandy, Sister Catherine Ignatia de la May, has returned to her convent after a spending spree in Paris that left her order, the Sisters of the Sacred Heart, both titillated and dismayed.

De la May is reported to have left the convent in Ry a week last Friday to visit a group of novices temporarily attached to the Ecole Normale Supérieure in central Paris. Due to arrive early that morning, she finally turned up eight hours late, having instead traversed the city in the company of an unusually large amount of cash, buying various fripperies that were intended, she later admitted, to 'please our Lord Jesus Christ and, in a roundabout way, myself'.

LUXURY

Her first stop, at Guerlain, just off the Boulevard St Germain, involved the testing of several luxury scents worth hundreds of euros. Georges Durand, who served Sister Catherine, said yesterday, 'She appeared to have a perfect "nose", as we say. I did of course wonder at the lady's mode of dress, but she seemed very charming, and certainly knew her aldehydes from her chypres. Utterly charming, in fact. It's some time since I studied my catechism but I don't recall there being any prohibitions on the wearing of fragrance in Holy Orders.'

Sister Catherine left the shop with a complimentary *flacon* of Vol de Nuit. 'Well, of course gifts are at the discretion of the manager,' said M. Durand, 'but the lady was quite delightful, and it is, I'm afraid, some time since I set foot inside church.' The well-groomed salesman added, with a Gallic shrug, 'And of course some of us remain superstitious.'

Next stop for 'Our Lady of Pleasure', as Sister Catherine has been dubbed by the French press, was the House of Dior, home of the British *enfant terrible* John Galliano. In an interview with *Le Monde* yesterday, Sister Catherine admitted that the main objective of her expedition was to find 'the perfect black skirt – modest, but well cut, you know?' Alas, the House of Dior could not provide the requisite garment, offering instead, from the current collection, a series of mock-French Revolutionary bustiers. 'I may like shopping, but that would hardly make me a *tricoteuse*,' Sister Catherine said. She added, 'No matter. One must admire their instincts, if also promise to say a decade for their souls.'

The search for the 'perfect black skirt' continued along the rue de Rivoli, where the nun visited Chanel's flagship store. Its chief *vendeuse*, Marie LaBarre, told the *Telegraph*, 'I was a little bit surprised at first to see a Sister in the shop – though, of course, black and white were Mademoiselle Chanel's preferred colours and so, in a way, Sister Catherine was in the right place. She has very perfect skin, I must say. When I asked her whether she used our cosmetic product range, she smiled and said, "only water and soap", but I'm not sure that I believed her.'

Sister Catherine tried on three skirts, all ankle-length, in silk dupion, which Mlle LaBarre described as being most suitable for evening wear; in Chanel's trademark tweed, which Sister Catherine apparently found too fussy; and, finally, in triple-dyed black flannel. 'There could be no doubting her excellent taste,' reported Mlle LaBarre. 'Only a connoisseur would opt for something so divinely understated.'

Sister Catherine purchased the skirt there and then. Following her success, she told *Le Monde*, she took herself to tea at the famous *salon de thé* Ladurée on the Left Bank. 'My niece has told me many times about the exceptional pistachio macaroons at Ladurée, and I couldn't resist. It was such a pleasure to get away from soups.'

After her now-celebrated day out, Sister Catherine found her way to the novices she had been due to visit that morning — her unusual lateness having prompted an anxious call to the police and a subsequent search. Responding to a hostile article in the left-leaning French daily *Citoyen*, which had drawn parallels between the nun's 'pleasure-seeking nature' and the 'insidious corruption of the Catholic Church', Mother Superior Bernadette Gourdot of the Sisters of the Sacred Heart, said, 'Sister Catherine has been an exemplary member of our community for over a dozen years. She is very popular here.

'Before joining us, she was, I believe, involved in the procuring of beads from India for the ornamentation of handbags. They were quite beautiful. In actual fact, Sister Catherine has of late put some of this fine knowledge to good use: our altar cloths and kneelers are of the most original design. We look forward to her safe return.'

And no possibility of punishment?

'Not all all,' said the Mother Superior. 'We shall all be happy to endure our punishments just as soon as we deserve them.'

As support poured in from all over France for Sister Catherine, born Delphine Lacoste, it briefly began to look as though we might be seeing more of the irrepressible nun. 'She should have her own cable show,' said the *Telegraph*'s fashion editor, Hilary Alexander. 'How about it — *Get the Habit*?'

But it seems there will be no further public performances for the apparently unabashed Sister Catherine. 'I had a lovely day,' she said yesterday, 'and I have my skirt now. But it is time for me to turn my attention to the spiritual development of the novices. Time is short, and we have much to learn.'

Acknowledgements

With particularly heartfelt thanks to Sam Wilson for the glorious illustrations, to Smith & Gilmour for the equally glorious design, and to Sophia Langmead for research. And to Georgia Garrett and Mrs P, as ever. They love the shops, those two.

Index

AAA Australia Shopping Mall 18, 107
ABC-inkjets 128
Abebooks 47
Abercrombie & Kent 144
acne 82
Agent Provocateur 185
Alchemy 92
Amanda Lacey 80, 82
Anne's House of Dreams 109
Annick Goutal 85, 87
Antoine & Lilli 183
Antwerp 10
Anusol 101
Apartment 5 Cosmetics 69
Après l'Ondée 84, 85
Arabella 108
Arabella Boxer's Book of English Food 47
Architectural Plants 140, 186
Argos 110, 114, 121, 124, 132
Art Luna Salon 97
Artisan Parfumeur, L' 86
Asda 13
Au Bonheur des Dames 164
Austen, Jane 108

babies
   clothes 12–13
   presents 179, 186
backgammon 181
Bal à Versailles 85
bargains 135
Barry's Tea 42
baths 125, 126
beanbags 110
beauty 81, 101
   cleansers 77–8, 80–81
   facialists 82–3
   hair 96–8
   hands 98–9
   naturally alluring 96–7
   pubic hair 100
   scent 84–5
   toners 82
   see also make-up
bed books 108–9
beds 112–14, 184, 186
Belgian chocolate 60, 61

Berry Bros & Rudd 38, 179, 184
Best of Morocco 144
Beststuff 123
BhS 133
bikes 51
Birkenstocks 12
Black Opal 69
blankets 110, 112, 179
bleaching 93
Blessing, The 108
Bliss World 45, 186
Bluebell 87
Bluepet 138
Boden 12, 104, 171, 186
body lotion 96
BodySlimmers 58–9
books 194
   about food 46–7
   for children 160, 181
   for lounging with 108–9
boots 107
Bourjois 69
Boxer, Arabella 47
bras 168, 169, 171
Bravissimo 168
bread 48
bread machines 33
Bread Shop 48
Brittany 144
brows 19, 20–21, 23, 91, 182
Bruern Stable Cottages 143
Brussels 3–4, 9, 10, 14, 55–6
bulbs 140
Burnett, Frances Hodgson 108
butchers 35
Buxtonfoods 48

C&A 164–5
Cabbages and Roses 136
cakes 48
candles 135, 184
card games 181
Caron 85
Cath Kidston 18, 112, 133
Cazalet Chronicle, The 108
CDWow! 182, 183
Celtic Sheepskin Co. 107, 110

210

Cetaphil 81
Chanel 85, 92, 206
charities 174
cheese 37, 56, 60
chemists 117
children
    clothes 11, 12–13, 14, 16–17, 164–8, 172
    presents 179–83
    toys 159–62
    vouchers 192
chocolate 60, 61, 62, 64
Choudhury, Farida 21
christenings 179
Clarins Beauty Flash Balm 101
Classic Roses 140
Classy Pets Boutique 138
Cleanse and Polish Hot Cloth Cleanser
    77–8, 80
cleansers 77–8, 80–81
clothes
    bras 168, 169
    children 11, 12–13, 14, 16–17, 164–8, 172
    for dressing up 179–80
    for lounging in 104
    men 26–7, 29, 30
    over size 12 170–71
    pregnancy 75–6
    wedding dresses 156–7
Constance Spry Cookery Book, The 46
Cookcraft 122
Cooking Shop, The 123
Cooking in Ten Minutes 46
Cook's Kitchen 122
Cooper, Jilly 109
cork 121
Cosmetic Connection 68
cosmetics see make-up
Côte d'Or 61
Creed 87
Crocus 140, 186
Cucina Direct 122
Cuir de Russie 85
cushions 110, 111, 184

D. R. Harris 42, 183, 194
Dalsouple 121
David Champion 136, 194
De Witte Lelie 10
Debenhams 133, 171
delis 36, 37
Delvaux 10
Dermablend 89
detox 45
Diane von Furstenberg 171

dinosaur eggs 180
Dior 92
Diptyque 135
Divertimenti 122, 186
dog mcuk 138
dogs 137, 138
Donald Russell 35
Don't Tell Alfred 108
Dr Hauschka 80–81, 82, 126
dressing up 179–80
drink
    hangover cures 42
    wine 38, 39, 179, 184
du Maurier, Daphne 108, 109
Duane Reade 69
Dujardin 14
duvets 114

Eastbrook Farm 35
eczema 81
Editions de Parfums Frédéric Malle
    see Frédéric Malle
Egg 104
Electra Bicycle Company 51
EMKaraoke 135, 183
engagement presents 186
Esperya 37
Estée Lauder 88
Eve Lom Cleanser 80
Everywine 39
Evolution 180
extraction facials 83
eyebrows 19, 20–21, 23, 91, 182
eyelashes 96
eyeliner 94

facial hair 24, 25
facials 81, 82–3, 182, 183, 184
Fairley, Josephine 67
farm shops 52
feet 99, 100
Feminité du Bois 85
Fernet Branca 42
Findus Crispy Pancakes 56
Fine Cell Work 111
Firebox 54
Fish Society 52
flooring 121
Florence 87
Floris 86
Flourbin 48
flowers 129, 130
food 32–3, 41, 43, 45, 47, 49, 53, 55–6
    books about 46–7

bread and cakes 48
butchers 35
delis 36, 37
online supermarkets 34
quinces 50
ready meals 40
vices 56–7
Forbo Nairn 121
Forever Amber 108, 182
Formes 75
Fortnum and Mason 180
foundation 77, 88
Fracas 85
France 144
Fraser, George MacDonald 181
Fray Bentos 56–7, 60
Frédéric Malle 86, 185, 194
Fresh Food Company 39
Fresh Water Filter Company 34
fridges 115, 183
Fromagerie, La 37

Galderma 81
Gap Kids 13
Garden Studios 127
gardens 137, 141
  nurseries, bulbs and seeds 140
GHD Ceramic Irons 98
Ghost 76, 171
Gieves and Hawkes 29
Godiva 60, 61
godparents 179–86
Gonzales, Bastien 100
Good Vibrations 73
Graham Kirkland 116
Grand Sophy, The 108
greed 43
Green Baby 13
Greggs the Baker 39
Grocer on Elgin 40
Guerlain 84, 85, 101, 205

hair 96–7, 182
  straightening irons 98
  weddings 156–7
  wigs 44
handbags 10
hands 98–9, 157, 189
Hands, Newby 68
hangover cures 42, 184, 186
Harper and Tom's 18, 130
Harpers & Queen 68
Harrods 85
Harry Duley 75–6, 104

Hawkin's Bazaar 54
Heaven @ home 186
Hennes & Mauritz 75
Heure Bleue, L' 84, 85
Heyer, Georgette 108
Hi-Waist BellyBuster 58–9
holiday rentals 144
holidays 143–4
home 119–22, 128–31, 136
  Argos 124
  bargains 132–3, 135
  baths 125, 126
  beds 112–14
  cushions, throws and blankets 110–12
  first 104, 106
  flowers 129, 130
  gardens 137
  kitchen equipment 121, 122–3
Homelink 144
hospital taps 125
House of Dior 206
house swaps 144
How to Eat 185, 186
Howard, Elizabeth Jane 108
Hypnos 113

I Capture the Castle 87, 108
Iceland 60
IKEA 133, 198
Insect Lore 162, 179, 180
Invitation to the Waltz 109
Ireland 144
Issey Miyake 76
Issima Midnight Secret 101
Italian Chapters 144
Italy 144

Jane 69
Jasmin 85
Jasmin Vert 85
Jean Desprez 85
Jekyll, Agnes 46
Jicky 85
Jo Malone 135
John Bell and Croydon 117
John Lewis 114, 122, 164
John Oliver 133
John Rocha 133
Jojo Maman Bébé 75
Jolene Cream Bleach 25
jwflowers 130

karaoke 134–5, 183
Kaviani, Arezoo 21

212 Keenmac Pubs 142, 195
Keepers Nursery 50, 186
kippers 52
kitchen equipment 121, 122–3, 186
Kitchen Essays 46
Kleinman, Heather 68
kohl 69, 74

L Boutique 18, 156
Labour and Wait 136
Lady, The 144
Lakeland 122
Landmark Trust 143
Laura Mercier 88, 89, 135
Lawson, Nigella 185, 186
Leaping Salmon 40, 186
Lehmann, Rosamond 109
Leonidas 61
Less Bounce 168
Letterbox 54
lighting 133
lino 121
lip-liners 92
lipstick 91–2
Lipstick Rose 86
Little Badger 12–13
Little Shrimp 13
Liz Earle 18, 77–8, 80, 82
London Review of Books 144
Longborough Farm Shop 52
loo paper 131, 133
Los Angeles 97
lounging 103, 106
    beds 112–14
    books 108–9
    clothes 104
    cushions, throws and blankets 110–12
    titchy fridges 115
    Ugg boots 107
Love in a Cold Climate 108
Lovely Me 67
Lush 80, 182

MAC 92
Madonna 98
Maître Parfumeur et Gantier 85
make-up 67–8, 69, 70, 74, 77, 184
    artists 150
    chic 91
    lipstick 92
    looking at least ten years older 94
    mascara 95
    perfect-seeming skin 88–90
    pulled together in a hurry 92

weddings 157
MakeupAlley 68, 85
Making of a Marchioness, The 108
Mandarin Oriental Spa 45
manicures 157, 189
Manon 64
Manufactum Ltd 128, 136, 194
mark-ups 198
Marks & Spencer 13, 40, 164, 165–6
Martin's Sea-Fresh Fish 52
mascara 95
Masqueraders, The 108
massages 186
Max Factor 69, 95
Maybelline 69
meat 35
Meg Rivers 18, 48, 181, 183
Melin Tregwynt 112, 183
men
    shirts 26–7, 29, 30
    shopping 8
Metallious, Grace 109
Midnight Secret 101
Miller Harris 85, 87
Mini Boden 12
mini-coolers 115, 183
Miss Pettigrew Lives for a Day 108, 194
Miss Selfridge 164, 166
missgroovy 96, 98
Mitford, Nancy 108
Mitsouko 85
moisturizer 81
Montgomery, L. M. 109
Morocco 144
motorbikes 26
Mouchoir de Monsieur 85
Much Depends on Dinner 47
muslin cloths 78
My Cousin Rachel 108, 109

Nancy Gantz 58–9
Narcisse Noir 85
Nars 92
National Trust 143
net-a-porter 171
Neuhaus 61, 64
New and Lingwood Ltd 29
Nicholas, St 53, 55
Nippaz With Attitude 12
nurseries 140

Ocado 34
office supplies 128
Officina Profumo-Farmaceutica di Santa

Maria Novella 87
Olympus Suite 100
online shopping 5–6, 197
  food and drink 32–3, 34, 35, 37, 39
Ordes Indes 85
organic box schemes 39
Otter Wrought Iron Products 49, 194

paint 132–3
Palmer's Cocoa Butter 96, 98
Pants of Steel 58–9, 171
Parker, Sarah Jessica 90
Parlett, David 181
Pashley Cycles 18, 51
Patel, Vashailly 20, 82
Paxton & Whitfield 37, 186
Pea in the Pod, A 75
pedicures 99, 100
Penguin Encyclopedia of Card Games, The 181
Penhaligon 87
perfume *see* scent
Persephone Books 46, 194
Pet 138
Peter Nyssen Ltd 140
Peyton Place 109
photographs 187–8
Pickett 18, 104, 181, 193, 194
playing cards 181
Pleats Please 76
Plumo 6
Pomiane, Edouard de 46
popbitch 98
Portobello Games 181
pot pourri 87
prairie oyster 42
pregnancy 74–6
Prescriptives 88
presents 174–8, 187–90, 193, 199
  for dads 194
  good godparent's guide 179–86
  for mums 194
  parents' wedding anniversary 195
  vouchers 191–2
Presents Direct 54
Prestat 62, 174
Prestige 69
Pride and Prejudice 108
Princess 16–17, 19
pubic hair 100
pubs 141, 142, 195
Puppy/Bedstock 18, 111, 184
Pure Cotton Comfort 13
Pursuit of Love, The 108
pyjamas 104, 186

Pym, Barbara 109

Quel Amour 85
quince jelly 49, 50
quinces 50

radios 184
ready meals 40
Real Charlotte, The 109
Refinery 42, 186
Regency Buck 108
religious goods 116
Relyon 113
REN 126
Renate 82
Richard James 29
Rigby and Peller 157
Ritchie's of Rothesay 52
Rococo 62
Rosebud Salve 69
roses 140
Ruby and Millie 69
Rural Retreats 143
Rykiel, Nathalie 73

Sainsbury's 34, 48
Sarah Raven's Cutting Garden 140
scent 84–5, 86–7, 182, 183, 185, 194, 205
seafood 49, 52
Seaman, Barbara 67
Secret Finish 90
seeds 140
Semmalina 12
Senteurs, Les 18, 86, 182, 183, 194
service 17–19, 197, 200
sex 71–2
sex aids 73
Sex and the City 90
Sh! 73
Shalimar 85
sheds 127
shirts 26–7, 29, 30
Shiseido 85
Silly Jokes 54, 181
Sisley 95
skin *see* beauty
Sleepyheads 104
Smile Place, The 93
Smith, Dodie 87, 108
Smith's Rosebud Salve 69
Snatch 181
Snugboots 107
sodium laureth sulphate 125

214

Somerville and Ross 109
Spa NK 45
spas 45, 186, 194
Spectator 144
Splendour 169, 185
Stacey, Sarah 67
Stamp, Terence 48
stationer's 4–5
stocking fillers 54
straightening irons 98
students 183
supermarkets 34, 184, 186, 197
Supertramp 141
Susann, Jacqueline 67
Swaddles Green Farm 35, 40

Tabac Blond 85
Tann-Rokka 136
taste 198
tea 42
teeth 93
Tesco 34
These Happy Golden Years 109
threading 20–21
throws 110, 112, 183
Toast 104
toilet paper 131, 133
toners 82
Topshop 171
Touche Éclat 90
Tourism Resources 144
toys 159–62
trampolines 141
Tree, Lady Anne 111
Trendco Hair Centre 44, 182
tuberose 85
Turnbull and Asser 29
21st Century Beauty Bible 67

Ugg boots 18, 107, 186
Ultrabland 80
underwear 157, 171, 185, 186
  bras 168, 169
  Pants of Steel 58–9
Urban Decay 69
Urban Zest 186

V. V. Rouleaux 188
Vaghela, Kamini 20
Valvona & Crolla 37
Vaseline 69
Vatel 3
Venice 144
Verhult's Fossils 180
Veronica Tomasso Cotgrove 144
Vi-Spring 112–13
Viking Direct 18, 128
Visser, Margaret 47
Vol de Nuit 85
vouchers 191–2

Waitrose 34, 37, 40
water 34
Watson, Winifred 108, 194
waxing 100
weathervanes 49, 194
wedding anniversaries 195
wedding dresses 156–7
wedding presents 114
weddings 147–54
wigs 44
Wilder, Laura Ingalls 109
Windsor, Kathleen 108, 182
wine 38, 39, 179, 184
Woman 73
Wooden Toy Catalogue 162

Yates, Paula 166
Yves Saint Laurent 92, 95

Zola, Emile 164